Memory Improvement, Accelerated Learning and Brain Training

Learn How to Optimize and Improve Your Memory and Learning Capabilities for Top Results in University and at Work

John Adams

© Copyright 2019 - All rights reserved.

The content contained within this book may not be reproduced, duplicated or transmitted without direct written permission from the author or the publisher.

Under no circumstances will any blame or legal responsibility be held against the publisher, or author, for any damages, reparation, or monetary loss due to the information contained within this book. Either directly or indirectly.

Legal Notice:

This book is copyright protected. This book is only for personal use. You cannot amend, distribute, sell, use, quote or paraphrase any part, or the content within this book, without the consent of the author or publisher.

Disclaimer Notice:

Please note the information contained within this document is for educational and entertainment purposes only. All effort has been executed to present accurate, up to date, and reliable, complete information. No warranties of any kind are declared or implied. Readers acknowledge that the author is not engaging in the rendering of legal, financial, medical or professional advice. The content within this book has been derived from various sources. Please consult a licensed professional before attempting any techniques outlined in this book.

By reading this document, the reader agrees that under no circumstances is the author responsible for any losses, direct or indirect, which are incurred as a result of the use of information contained within this document, including, but not limited to, — errors, omissions, or inaccuracies.

Table of Contents

Introduction – Know Your Brain   7

Chapter 1 – Memory: An Evidence Of Your Existence   15
- *What is Memory?*   15
- *Why Do We Forget?*   20

Chapter 2 - Memory Types and Their Need   25
- *Types of Memories*   25

Chapter 3 – Memory Preferences and Brain Waves: Accelerating Your Learning Channels   33
- *Different Memory Preferences a Person Can Have*   33
- *Brain Waves – Different States of Your Mind and Learning Capacity*   39

Chapter 4 – Visual Mnemonics: Tools & Techniques   47
- *The Journey Method*   47
- *Linking*   50
- *The Memory Palace*   55

Chapter 5 – Verbal Mnemonics: Tools & Techniques   65
- *Coding mnemonics*   65
- *Acronyms or Chunking*   67

Chapter 6 – Food for Your Memory   71
- *How Sugar Impacts Your Brain*   79

Chapter 7 – Physical Fitness for Improved Memory and Brain Function   83
- *The Golden Combination of Physical and Mental Exercise*   88

Chapter 8 – The Importance and Influence of Sleep   93

Sleep hygiene tips for quality sleep regularly   *95*

Myths about Sleep and Memory   *99*

Chapter 9 – Studying Hard Is Old School, Study Smart for Exams   103

Chapter 10 – Bring Your A-game at Work   109

How to keep your mind sharp at work?   *109*

Chapter 11 – Mistakes and Learning: How to Get Fastest Results   119

Perfectionism and Psychological Distress   *121*

How to Use Mistakes When Learning   *123*

Key takeaways   *127*

Chapter 12 – What You May Not Be Aware Of   129

Conclusion – Final Words   137

References   143

Introduction – Know Your Brain

Have you ever felt the fascination of reading printed words?

Not so fascinating? It is if you think about the million other things that happen at the same time in your body.

While you comprehend the written words, your heart keeps on beating, and you can feel the air on your skin. Your eyes know when to blink, and your lungs keep on breathing for you.

There is one headquarter where all of it is controlled at once.

That headquarter is your brain.

Your brain gives the needed rhythm to your heart, controls the temperature, and does a billion other things. In addition, you can read and remember what you have read too.

Every activity, which you can or cannot control, is managed by your brain. That is why your brain does not sleep. Even when you are in your bed giving yourself a good night's sleep, your mind keeps on working. Your brain helps you get a sound sleep. Shutting down unnecessary activities, repairing cells and keeping the crucial events in check. These are a few of many jobs your brain does when you go to sleep.

How Does Your Brain Work?

Your brain has three major areas:

- Cerebrum
- Cerebellum

- Brain Stem

The most significant part of your brain, with two left and right divisions, is called cerebrum. This part of your mind controls your thinking ability, language comprehension, eating, memories, senses, drinking, body temperature, sleeping, and hormones.

Inside the cerebrum, you have your cerebellum, which is not more than a pear in size. But the job of this section is vital. Your muscle movements are managed here. In addition, your ability to coordinate your body functions also comes from here.

Your brain has its extension to your body through the spinal cord, which makes the complete nervous system of your body. Neurons in your brain are 100 billion, creating a vast network in your whole body.

How Do We Learn Things?

Learning is how any living organism survives. We, as humans, have enhanced learning abilities in the living kingdom, so improved that we have not even understood it all yet. Our genetics and surroundings decide what we learn and how fast we can learn those things.

For example, if you read a chapter of your book every day, eventually your brain will adapt to this activity. Your reading ability will improve, and you will start remembering most sentences of that chapter.

Similarly, a worker, who has to attach the right information label to the right product, gets efficient with his or her work with practice. It all happens due to our brain's ability to learn and adapt to new things.

There is no doubt that learning is the most critical skill your brain offers. You can improve your verbal intelligence, enhance your working memory, learn new languages and do more; all because your mind lets you do so.

Every time you stretch your abilities, your brain network changes substantially to help you adapt. That is why something that seems impossible becomes more straightforward day-by-day. Moreover, eventually, you get comfortably efficient doing that activity.

At the beginning of learning something new, your brain has to put an effort to concentrate and control. Practice trains your mind to adjust networks on a large scale. Therefore, with time, the effortful activity of the brain reduces, and the new system manages the operation on its own. That is how things get simple to remember, and actions get more comfortable for you. That is the process of how your brain reaches the automated level of skill. The brain activity enhances every time you practice something, which tends to improve the effortlessness.

Let us dive into the technicality of learning things.

Practicing an activity increases a synapse's strength in your brain. Two neurons keep being activated repeatedly. That creates a permanent link between those two neurons. This process is known as long-term potentiation. Because of this process, every time, the first of the two neurons is activated, it automatically activates the second one.

Researches on rats have shown that learning new things also increases the size of the brain. New protrusions, known as dendritic spines, get larger to help a rat find food through a tunnel during experiments.

Briefly, our brain develops more neuron connections, we learn more, and that learning becomes permanent information stored in our brain network. We have to think less when remembering or doing something.

Can We Enhance Our Learning Abilities?

"Believe in yourself" - you must have heard that a thousand times from your peers, your parents, and teachers. How about you modify this and make it-

"Believe in your brain."

Your brain can learn anything and become a master of that skill. From understanding complex data every day, to memorizing a long list of formulas for exams, you can do it all. Just put your faith in the brain and neuron network it has up there in your head.

The science of how the brain learns is all about facts, so you can believe in that and give yourself a chance to learn anything you like. Nevertheless, it is not only related to understanding the scientific concepts, but it is also linked to applying that science to lets your brain learn efficiently.

There is an external process as well as an internal process of learning. The external means such as training, guides, tutorials, and others help you begin the learning process. These are great during the initial phase, but you have to go beyond and allow your brain to practice internally. If you are getting information without practicing to solve tasks or problems, it will not help. Your mind requires actual tasks to practice and build strong neuron networks. Therefore, you need to ACTUALLY do it and fail a thousand times to become a master.

Using failure for productivity

You must have heard this a thousand times - experiencing a failure and overcoming it makes you stronger. If that is true, you can utilize failure to improve your productivity.

For example, a university student can work on math problems, without understanding the concepts in the first place. The student can look at the question first, then, analyze the ideas to find out a way to reach the right answer. However, getting the correct answer is not the ultimate goal here. This approach helps in finding out new ideas about the problem. It is also possible to find a new way of solving that question. The work approach for such type of questions will become more comfortable for the student. Hence, it will enhance productivity. That is how you utilize failure for productivity.

Similarly, suppose you have a new machine you need to work on, which comes with a user manual. Instead of using the instructions, you can figure out the functions on your own. You will try to fail, but a personal quest for the right solution stays in your mind for a long time. You sustainably learn things.

Another important thing about the learning ability is the period you choose. Most people tend to involve too much in their learning process, once they get a grip of their concentration. However, an obsessive approach to learning only gives you a temporary solution.

To learn and retain knowledge, you should focus on choosing a longer period of learning. Spreading the learning process allows your brain to form long-term networks of neurons. Students of every age utilize this approach without even knowing it. The habits of revising chapters, quizzing and other methods are popular to learn and retain knowledge. Just distribute this approach within a long period, and you can enhance your learning ability.

The science behind distributed learning is pure. You give sensations to similar neuron networks from time to time by practicing something. Your brain receives stimulations in small and short sessions, which is why the process of skill development and learning becomes more comfortable. Therefore, instead of giving 4 hours to a project in one day, you can give 15 to 20 minutes every day and master it in a week.

Your senses and learning

Experiences become memories, and every thought in your body gives you a unique ability to experience things. Your eyes give the experience of sight, your ears let you experience hearing, skin gives a background of touch, and you smell with your nose and taste with your tongue.

Think about it, if you once sip a very hot coffee, your brain stores that experience as a memory. So, when the next time you are about to have a sip, your brain tells you to be cautious. That is how your senses assist in creating a memory, which becomes learning. The more feelings are involved in an experience, the better the mind it creates. That is why students, who look at the text and say it aloud, revise more effectively.

If an action is happening in your head only, it stays virtual. Only your artistic skills are enhanced with virtual experiences. The brain creates neuron networks when you provide real-world experiences. Therefore, using your skills in real life is very important. Use a foreign language and work on your data evaluation method daily. That is how you can learn and retain that knowledge as well.

When bringing your rehearsal approach to the real world, context matters too. Your brain gives importance to learning things, which becomes a matter of your survival. For example, your accounting skills will get stronger and faster if you use it to manage your taxes, savings, and investments. Your brain knows that finances matter to you. Hence, you will learn faster.

How can one define memory? How do they work inside our minds?

Through this book, you will have a better grasp about its fundamentals and workability. By the end of this book, you will find yourself more familiar with this world of memories and the functioning of the brain activity.

Brief Introduction about Your Memory

Everything that you are is a collection of memories stored in your mind. Every second, you are creating new memories and using them. You store them in your mind and can recall whenever required.

From brushing your teeth in the morning to remembering complex information related to your projects, you do it all.

The human memory is a center of fascination for scientists, psychologists, and philosophers. But, understanding your ability to create memories can help you too.

You already know how experiences help in memory creation and memories let you learn effectively. So, if you see the process of memory creation, memory storage, and its organization, you can increase your brain capacity.

So, let us talk about memory in detail!

Chapter 1 – Memory: An Evidence Of Your Existence

Your memory is your way of understanding the surroundings. Every time you experience something, your brain tries to make sense of it by looking at the stored memory. If no memory is available, it creates a new consciousness and stores. The process happens every second, which builds your personality, knowledge, and skills.

So, it would not be wrong to say that your memory is the evidence of your existence.

What is Memory?

In an overview, a memory is a process through which your brain acquires, stores and recalls information. There are different types of memories, making this process extremely complex to study.

Three memory processes include:

1. Encoding- obtaining an information
2. Storage- storing that information
3. Retrieval- recalling that information

Unfortunately, human memory is full of flaws. We tend to forget things or remember things differently. In many situations, we encode the memory incorrectly, which disturbs the other two processes. Most issues with losing memory are minor, such as leaving your car keys, forgetting to switch off the lights and others. However, complex flaws in the ability to create memories can result in mental diseases and have a huge impact on someone's life.

Formation of Memory

Your experiences encompass millions of minor and significant details. It is all information for your brain. For working without breaking down, your mind decides to filter information and prioritize memory creation. That is why info has to be useful to become a memory in the first place. If your brain thinks that information is not helpful for you, it tends to forget it.

That is the reason why some students do not seem to remember the concepts taught during classes. It is all about how interested you are at retaining information.

Once you make information usable, it gets encoded as a memory in your brain. Then the storage process occurs, which allows your mind to store that memory. However, you do not stay aware of the stored memory, unless you recall it. That is exactly like working on a project and saving it in a digital folder. You do not keep remembering the data in your head 24/7, but it comes back as soon as you have a purpose for it. That is what retrieval of memory is.

The storage and retrieval of memories are the reasons why you have conscious and unconscious awareness. The storage process keeps the minds in your unconscious perception, and the retrieval process brings it back the conscious awareness, whenever you require.

But, as said before, it all depends on the quality of information encoding.

The Period of Existence of a Memory

Your brain has a wide diversity when it comes to creating and keeping memories. Some memories last for a fraction of a second, while others stay with you for years. That is logical, as you would not want to remember the name of a restaurant forever, where you only went once to have a meal. Every time you walk on a busy road, your brain sees every tiny sign, numbers, people's faces, their dress color, and a billion other things. All these pieces of information can be important right at that moment. However, you will not need them longer than a fraction of a second. That is why the diversified period of existing memory matters.

Memories can be as brief as a fraction of a second. Your senses provide information about the surroundings, and your brain uses them to help you handle a situation.

There are short-term memories as well, which last for about 20 to 30 seconds. You think about something or focus on certain information, which turns into short memories. That can also be the encoding process. The importance of a short-term memory decides whether it can become long-term memory. If not, they fade away in the vast mental database in your brain.

When you obtain important information, it can stay as a stored memory for days, months and even years. These memories remain in your unconscious and come to the conscious awareness when you recall. The period of existence depends on how many times you keep recalling a memory.

For example, if you are revising a chapter for an upcoming test, the encoded memories can last for weeks and months, depending on the revision. However, you start losing the grip after the test. That is why regular revision becomes necessary. On the other hand, a memory of a date with your partner can stay for months and years.

Memory Retrieval – How It Works

Memory retrieval is precisely what a student does during an exam to answer questions given. The same process is tried on a daily basis in the life of knowledge workers, data analysts, and managers.

The success of memory retrieval depends on the cues available in the surroundings. Useful signals trigger the retrieval process, which successfully brings the memory back to conscious awareness.

Depending on the cue or clue, memory retrieval has four types:

- **Recalling**

Recalling is the process when you retrieve memory in the absence of any evidence or signal. The surroundings do not help in triggering the retrieval, so, you have to rely on your ability to bring back a memory. This type of retrieval takes place when you are making a test or giving a presentation in front of your seniors.

- **Recollection**

You recollect a memory when the surroundings offer you some clues in the form of logical structures. Partial information stays available, which triggers the process of memory recollection. For example, if a test contains essay or passage questions, it allows a student to utilize the given information to remember the rest of it. Hence, he or she can answer these questions. Recollecting memory is usually easier than memory recall.

- **Recognition**

In some cases, you have all the information hidden in the surroundings. The brain allows you to recognize the right information by triggering its memory. For instance, a test with multiple choice questions gives the correct answer along with other options. A student needs to recognize the right answer. Similarly, if you reach a street, which you visited years ago, your recognition of that street will help you take the right turns.

- **Relearning**

Relearning something enables you to retrieve the stored memories. Every time you relearn, it strengthens your ability to recover that memory. That is the reason why you do not have to learn the whole chapter when revising it. An overview allows your brain to retrieve all the memory encoded in the first place.

The Three Stages of Memory

First introduced by Shiffrin and Atkinson in 1968, there is a stage model that divides memories into three stages.

- **Sensory memory**

This memory stage usually involves visual and auditory information. Generally, visual information lasts for 1/2-second only. On the other hand, you can keep auditory details for 3 to 4 seconds. The brain gives prioritized importance to sensory memories. Just a few of these memories move to the next stage of memories.

- **Short-term or conscious memory**

This stage is also called active consciousness or your conscious mind, things that you are presently thinking about or aware of. They are the part of your dynamic memory. Sensory memories are created automatically. But, when you start focusing on particular sensory memory, it becomes a short-term or active memory. These memories last for about 20-30 seconds. Then, most of these memories fade away. However, if you are attentive enough, some active mind reaches the next stage.

- **Long-term or unconscious memory**

Long-term memory includes memories that you are not working with but may want in future. The stored memory is also known as unconscious memory. That is because they stay outside the present awareness of your mind. But whenever required, the memory comes back to your consciousness.

Why Do We Forget?

Forgetting is a common flaw in the process of human memory generation and retrieval. We tend to forget things.

An ideal memory would never let you forget anything that you experience. Imagine that! You will not have to read one chapter twice to memorize it or struggle with the same information every day as a data manager. This flaw is the reason why we all have to work on our ability to remember essential things more efficiently.

But, do not take forgetting as an error. It is a flaw, but a beneficial one. Your brain needs space to perform without breaking down. That is why it tries to forget and remember for various reasons. Time is one of the biggest reasons that triggers forgetting. Information fades away if you do not bring it to your consciousness with rehearsal.

There are four fundamental reasons why we tend to forget things:

1. Failing to retrieve

2. Interference among memories

3. Failing to store

4. Deliberate forgetting

- **Failing to retrieve**

How many times have you felt that your brain has wholly forgotten something? Or you have the information somewhere in there, but it is not coming to the conscious mind. That is known as retrieval failure.

If you are unable to retrieve a memory, it can mean two things:

- You have not been practicing that memory lately.
- You do not give importance to that memory.

Mostly, time vanishes memories or reduces its print in our brain. This happens if you do not practice or retrieve a memory from time to time.

On the other hand, some memories stay intact even if you do not rehearse them. This occurs when a long-term memory is too important to forget for your brain.

- **Interference among memories**

Another reason why you forget is the interference among your memories. This takes place when you store new memories that overlap or contradict existing memories.

There are two situations when your memories can interfere with each other:

- Old memory is so strong that you feel unable to remember a new one similar to that. This is called proactive interference. For example, if a knowledge worker processes the same type of data for years, it becomes a strong memory. Hence, such a worker has to work hard to memorize a new process of working on a different data set.

- A new memory contradicts or competes with an old memory making the retrieval difficult. This phenomenon is called retroactive interference. For example, a student can learn the wrong approach to solving a problem. But, when the right path becomes visible, it interferes with the process learned previously.

- **Failing to store**

In many conditions, you cannot remember something because you have not encoded its memory correctly. If memory did not reach the long-term stage, it is impossible to remember it.

This also happens due to the prioritization of details conducted by your brain. For example, to remember a way to your classroom, you do not have to remember the color of the wall in the hallway. Only important details are stored by our brain to make long-term memory useful and reliable.

But, the same thing can divert your attention and lead to incorrect or no information stored about an experience. Hence, you cannot seem to retrieve that information in the future.

- **Deliberate forgetting**

Sometimes, we forget things because we want to. This usually happens to the memories associated with disturbing events or traumatic experiences. Our brain knows the anxiety we feel when a bad memory comes back to conscious awareness. To minimize the trauma, your mind takes charge and eliminates those pieces of information. The process involves suppression of memory to unconscious storage and forgetting it altogether.

There are arguments regarding the concept of suppressed memories. However, that is mostly because of the difficulty of studying memories, which are not detectable in the first place.

Forgetting things is not entirely avoidable. But, now that you have the reasons attached to it, you would know why you have forgotten something. Also, you can look at informational pieces critically and decide how likely you would forget or remember them. If a memory seems difficult to recognize, you can work on rehearsing and practicing it regularly and keeping it a part of your retrieval memory.

Chapter 2 - Memory Types and Their Need

You have already gained a glimpse of memory types in the previous chapter. However, there are more types, and every class has its importance in your everyday life.

Types of Memories

Human memory has three main stages according to the Atkinson-Shiffrin model:

- Sensory memory
- Short-term memory
- Long-term memory

Modern studies have given sub-divisions of long-term memories. But first, let's understand how sensory memory works.

Sensory Memory

Lasting for about 1/2-second, you get sensory memory from your ability to see, hear, smell, touch, and taste. These memories form to offer an instant understanding of the environment. Hence, their purpose is lost within a fraction of a second. You deliberately ignore these memories, or your brain forgets them automatically.

Short-term memory

When you actively pay attention to something, it becomes a part of your short-term memory. You focus on sensory memories to increase their existence period to 20-30 seconds. That is how short-term memories come into existence.

In an overview:

- Short-term memories do not require active maintenance as they last for 20-30 seconds only.

- You can just think about seven or so things at once, which limits the short-term memory.

Period of a short-term memory

The period of short-term memory is increasable to 1 minute or so. This is possible through active working or rehearsing the memory. For example, people keep repeating a new phone number until they find a piece of paper to write it down. Without constant repetition, you are more likely to forget a new phone number within seconds.

Even the repetition or rehearsal can take your short-term memory to a certain extent only. After 1 minute or so, your existing memories start interfering with the short-term information.

Using the phone number example again, if you do not find a piece of paper early enough, your brain will start recalling other phone numbers stored in your long-term memory. The old memories will interfere and displace the new memory, and you will forget the phone number.

With enough time given to the rehearsal of short-term memory, you can move it to the long-term stage.

The capacity of your short-term memories

You can have about 5-9 items in your short-term memory. Beyond that, your brain starts getting confused and losing track of thoughts.

Your short-term memory is a bit different from the working memory you have. While short-term memories provide temporary information storage, working memories allow you to collect, organize and rearrange information temporarily.

So, working memory is a temporary form of long-term memory process. In addition, short-term memory is a part of your working memory.

Long-term memory

Your long-term memory stores information in your unconscious awareness and allows you to use them whenever required. This storage requires maintenance with practice and rehearsal to keep the stored memories detailed. However, some memories stay fresh even after months and decades without practicing them at all.

So, there are two types of long-term memories your brain works with:

1. Explicit memory

You generate an explicit memory by consciously practicing something. For example, if you memorize a phone number or your credit card pin, it would become a part of your explicit memory.

Now, there is a type of explicit memory, which is known as declarative memory. This memory type includes all the factual information pieces. For example, when you recall faces, event dates, or instructions about a game, they come from the declarative memory storage.

Declarative memory has three types too:

- **Episodic memory** - This includes recalling all the facts associated with your experiences in a sequence. Such memories are usually related to times, emotions, places or things that have contextual importance.

- **Semantic memory** - Semantic memory is more structured as compared to episodic memories. This type includes facts, knowledge, concepts and other structural information your brain stores. Regardless of the presence of personal context, you remember things as facts through this memory type.

- **Autobiographical memory** - While episodic memory can include event memories in a sequence, autobiographical memory stores events that are more personal. This type of memory is usually similar to the episodic memories. However, it involves more individual events, instead of a sequence of events.

2. *Implicit memory*

Implicit is a more unconscious form of memory that impacts your behavior or thoughts. You do not remember a memory, but it changes the way you behave or think. For instance, your childhood memory of certain places does not come back. But if you see that place again, you know where to go. That is what an implicit memory does to you.

There are two types of implicit memories:

- **Procedural memory** - This memory allows you to remember actions and tasks. Your skill in doing something is called the procedural memory. So, you know how to brush your teeth, drive or wear clothes.

- **Emotional memory** - Certain implicit memories can trigger emotional responses. The emotions can come along with procedural and declarative processes.

Interesting Facts about Long-term Memories

1. **Long-term memories mostly stay outside your conscious awareness.** Most often, you recall your long-term memories in the working memory zone to utilize them for a purpose. In some situations, you have control over recalling, while other times the process occurs on its own due to environmental cues.

2. **Frequently accessed and used memories are more likely to stand strong in front of time.** The memories you recall become powerful. But all the memories that are not retrieved become weaker with time. Usually, our brain tends to replace old, unwanted memories with new ones.

How a Short-term Memory Becomes A Long-term Memory

Due to the minor duration of short-term memory, important memories are transferred to the long-term collection of memories.

One common approach is memorizing information in chunks. This method is a memory training approach, which you utilize to learn things in small segments. For example, a manager can divide informational pieces into groups. Each group can contain a similar set of information. This way, memorizing becomes easier.

If you have a list of 10 formulas, learning them in sets of two would seem easier than memorizing them separately.

Rehearsal is also a valid option to turn short-term memories into long-term memories. You revise, review and analyze information repeatedly. This gives your brain a chance to remember things for a long time. This approach, however, requires consistent rehearsal from time to time. Students, managers and knowledge workers can utilize this approach to make everyday memory sharper and retain critical information.

According to the Atkinson-Shiffrin model, all-important short-term memories become long-term, automatically. The duration of long-term memories also differs regarding their importance and practice. Working on your neural networks certainly helps in improving your ability to store long-term memories and accurately retrieving them.

How A Long-term Memory Changes

To understand memory in your brain, you can think about the memory of a computer. Information is stored in a computer's hard disk and retrieved whenever required. The same thing happens in our brain. Different environmental cues trigger just the retrieval.

Every time you retrieve your memory, it changes. This is a common concept of information processing. You recall information and work on it, which tends to change the form of that long-term memory. This happens due to the upgrades provided to the same neural networks every time you recall a memory. Your long-term memory becomes a part of working memory, which begins the encoding process again.

This shows that you can change your long-term memories, for better or worse. Details can change, and you can improve or weaken your memories. It all depends on what you do with memory after recalling it.

There is another reason why long-term memories change-interference. Your brain does not keep memories in a static form. So, it can't give you back an exact piece of memory every time you recall. So, to resolve this flaw, the brain searches for similar memories to fill the gaps in the required memory. This can fill memory with misinformation and interfere with the stored long-term memory. So, you tend to believe that you are right when you are not.

How many times have you thought you answered a question correctly, but it was not the case? It is common among students. You mix information in your head and create new information, which seems right.

Visualization and Memory Techniques

With the clarity that long-term memories do change, you need to work on memory training to save yourself from memory interference. Visualization is the best approach to remembering things correctly.

When you see images, it helps your brain collect every tiny detail associated with it. So, retrieving visual memories becomes easier and accurate. This is probably the reason why most memory tools and techniques utilize the visualization power of the brain. Most techniques give weird imagery to help people memorize situations and sequences faster.

A great visualization capacity of a person is called a photographic memory.

A person with photographic memory holds the ability to retain and recall detailed visual information accurately.

It is popular that a person with photographic memory stores memories in the form of still imagery. Therefore, whenever recalling, this person can look at the details of that image memory in his or her mind and recollect information. However, that is not the actual way photographic memory works.

To experiment, you can ask a person with a photographic memory to remember text on a page and rewrite it backwards, using his or her photographic memory. No one can do this.

As you already know, our memories are not a static collection. They are like pieces of puzzles stored in a box. So, when a person recalls a memory, he or she utilizes different puzzle pieces to create the whole picture. Small bits of memories are easy to store and easy to retrieve which is what our brain does to collect information in long-term memory efficiently. This ability to collect and retrieve memory pieces can differ from person to person. We all have different attentive personalities, which tends to divert the ability to look at the details when collecting information. But, at the same time, it is also possible to improve your photographic memory by working on visual techniques and tools.

Overall, visualization is a great way of remembering information. The memory does not work like still photographs, but it can collect small bits of imagery like separate informational pieces. So, you can utilize images to enhance your ability to remember things.

Chapter 3 – Memory Preferences and Brain Waves: Accelerating Your Learning Channels

Different Memory Preferences a Person Can Have

Our surroundings offer us different kinds of information. We obtain information via sight, sound, and feeling. These different types of memories are known as:

- **Visual memory** - what you see, such as facial expressions, printed materials, body language, and more.
- **Auditory memory** - what you hear or say, such as sounds, spoken words, and more.
- **Kinesthetic memory** - what you feel, such as actions, emotions, smell, taste, movement, and others.

However, we are not equally sensitive to all three types of memory channels. One person's memory preference can differ from another.

In humans, about 40% of people get more memories through visuals. About 30-40% remember feelings, which is a form of kinesthetic memory. Lastly, about 20-30% people memorize through the auditory channel.

So, we all have our preferences when it comes to memorizing. Or, you can say that your mind has a choice when it comes to learning things. Finding your most sensitive memory channel can help in memory improvement and accelerated learning. This is true for everyone: from a knowledge worker, a manager to a university student. After all, we all have to memorize and deal with memories.

Visual Memory – Are You More Sensitive To What You See?

From college to career, your visuals constantly help you memorize things. Visual memory assists in learning activities, skills and allows you to form short-term as well as long-term memories.

Visual memory is your ability to recall memories in the form of imagery. If you are sensitive to visuals, your memories often include images. For example, a student with visual memory preference can visualize the text written on the pages of his or her book when remembering.

For a visual sensitive person, short-term memory stays full of imagery. It is like your brain clicks pictures all the time and allows you to store them in your neuron networks for a few seconds. People who lack visual memory tend to forget visuals very quickly. For example, such a student might struggle when copying notes due to not being able to collect and store short-term visual memories.

Your long-term memories also contain small puzzle pieces in the form of imagery. People with a strong visual memory tend to recollect imagery even after months or years. Generally, we all utilize visual memory to remember directions to our office or college.

The concept of a photographic memory has come from the visual memory only. If you look at an image, it allows your brain to look at the details regarding objects, sizes, depth, color, shadows, and other components. That is how a visual sensitive person looks at the world. He or she keeps on storing small pieces of images as groups of memories. Hence, when recalled, all the right pieces are aligned together in the brain, and a visual appears in a person's mind.

As the imagery is stored in pieces, the chances of clearly remembering the whole memory are not 100%. It depends on how sensitive you are to visuals. The degree of remembering visuals differs from person to person.

Why should you work to accelerate visual memory?

If you are a student, a knowledge worker or a manager, you constantly have to work on visual materials. Charts and diagrams are the realities of modern-age study and work environment. Visualized data is used to make the analysis process quicker and effective. You might spend time comparing diagrams, creating concept maps, and doing other tasks that require visual memory.

If you are a student of biology, you need to have a clear and strong visual memory to identify body parts. You have to learn and remember different muscles, bones, organs and other parts of the body. You need a strong visual memory brain training to become a successful doctor.

When you study statistics and look at concepts, your visual memory allows you to interpret the correct meaning. If visual memory is not exercised enough, your ability to make sense of a visualized data will reduce with time.

You have to have visual memory to clearly understand a lecture. Why? A professor, when giving a lecture, makes different postures and changes his or her facial expressions. You need to understand these visual clues to learn the concept taught during a lecture.

Similarly, you need visual sensitivity at every step of your life. Even if it is not your memory preference, you should indulge in brain training to increase your visual memory.

Auditory Memory – How Much Do You Remember From What You Hear?

Auditory memory is another sensory memory type. Your sense of hearing receives various sounds, and turns them into electrical charges. That charge reaches your brain via neuron networks, where sound images are created. Sound images are a type of mental concept created with sound.

Depending on your sensitivity, your brain can replay sound memories for a small period. Common examples of auditory memory include:

- Your ability to remember someone's name in one attempt.
- Listening to music and remembering the notes and words.
- Replaying other people's voices in your mind.

We listen and interpret other people's voices

Every time you listen to someone, you interpret that person's voice. Just like the facial expressions and body language, the tone of voice says a lot about a conversation. Our mind allows us to understand people by figuring out their voice tones. Some people have more sensitivity towards this mental ability and tend to remember voices for a long time.

Suppose your friend is telling all about his happy mood, but you still know that he is not happy. How? The words are all right, but your brain is catching on the facial expressions as well as the anxiousness in his voice tone. Similarly, you figure out when a person is angry, sad, happy, nervous or concerned. This ability is a superpower no matter what you do in your life. From personal, educational to professional life, you can grab every opportunity and behave appropriately by knowing how a person is feeling.

If you have a strong auditory memory, you can remember people's voices from just one conversation. When people call, you instantly figure out who that person is just by hearing their voice. Surely, this is common when you spend a lot of time with someone. However, auditory sensitivity enhances this ability, and you remember most voices you hear.

We all have a musical memory

Both musicians and non-musicians can have musical memory. Some people remember music better than others. This is also a sign of auditory memory preference. Musicians tend to remember the tone of instruments, different pitches, and tunes. Non-musicians, who enjoy listening to music, remember their favorite songs, its tune, and words altogether.

We recognize non-musical sounds

An experienced mechanic can hear the sound of your car's engine and recognize the problem. Not every mechanic can do that, but some develop higher sensitivity toward auditory memory. Their brain allows them to collect a new sound image and match it with an old image of the same kind. Hence, they figure out if your car has trouble or not.

Can you learn with your auditory memory?

Short answer - **YES.**

However, it depends on how attentive you are to sounds. For example, most students read and memorize, but tend to forget their lectures immediately. They either remember a few things or do not remember anything at all. However, some students tend to remember everything explained during a lecture. Students with high auditory memory tend to listen more and do not give too much importance to making notes. They simply want to focus on hearing every word uttered by the lecturer.

It is exactly like remembering the dialogues of your favorite TV series. But, just like a TV program, visuals help the audio too. For example, it is difficult to figure out the difference between "Won" and "One" if you do not have any context or visuals to help you.

There are auditory brain training tools for accelerated learning using audio approach. So, yes, you can learn effectively with the help of auditory memory. You would require improving this memory. The key is increasing the storage and retention capacity of sounds in your mind.

Kinesthetic Memory – Do You Remember What You Feel?

With Kinesthetic memory, you tend to remember a feeling of something. It is a comprehensive awareness of your physical and mental presence. The movements of your body, even tiny muscular movements become a part of your memory. The more sensitive you are towards movements and feelings, the higher your ability to make and retain kinesthetic memory.

With heightened kinesthetic memory, you tend to store

experiences regarding emotions or movements. This memory helps in learning activities such as typing faster or feeling the excitement of data evaluation. If you like to walk every time you read, it is associated with your kinesthetic memory. You have associated learning chapters with your movement of walking. Hence, it helps you memorize things faster.

People with a strong kinesthetic memory tend to move a lot. Moving legs, tapping the pen on the table and other movements keep their brain and memory active which is why physical tasks become easier for such learners. If one of your hobbies include physical activity such as sports, running, dancing, swimming or anything else, it means you have a heightened sense of kinesthetic.

Kinesthetic memory creates coordination between your body and the space around it. That increases body and mind coordination and offers you faster reactions.

Brain Waves – Different States of Your Mind and Learning Capacity

Everything you feel comes from the mental state created by the certain waves in your brain. The feeling of happiness, sadness, and other emotions depend on brain waves. Understanding and controlling brain waves are necessary to learn anything. Certain mental states are better to learn faster, while some do not allow you to focus.

Most people spend their lives thinking that it is the external world changing their personalities. So, if you are not able to memorize a chapter, it is because of the upsetting thing your girlfriend said earlier that day. Sure, external elements send information to your brain, but you can control how to deal with that information. Your mindset, beliefs, and thoughts are just common results of brain waves.

In your brain, neural waves create different conscious states. Therefore, if you know those states, you can work on them and control your mindset more effectively.

Your mental state depends on 5 kinds of brain waves:

1. Alpha waves - for deep relaxation at 7.5 to 14 Hz

When you close your eyes, your mind reaches a level of relaxation. This state occurs when you daydream or meditate. You can look at it as a light meditative state when your mind generates alpha waves. These waves increase the visualization of your mind. Your memory creating skills heighten, you learn faster and imagine vividly.

Alpha waves put you right at the gate of your subconscious. So, you can stay conscious and concentrate better to maximize your ability to learn. Your intuitions become stronger and stronger as you get closer to the maximum state of alpha waves at 7.5 Hz.

2. Beta waves - for reasoning and awaken consciousness at 14 to 40 Hz

Brainwaves on beta scale allow you to stay alert and awake. Your consciousness stays logical and obtains the ability to critically reason and evaluate the surroundings.

Beta waves help you go through all the tasks during any day. However, these are the waves that let you feel anxious, restless and stressed-out.

When you have beta waves running in your brain, it becomes

your inner critic. The loudness of this critical voice depends on the strength of beta waves in your brain. The stronger the waves, the higher stressed you feel during a day. Most students and professionals function with beta waves and stay stressed out.

3. Theta waves - for sleeping and light meditation at 4 to 7.5 Hz

Beyond alpha state, you reach a light sleeping stage of theta waves. These brain waves also create a state of dream. Achieving theta waves in your brain can help you develop a strong spiritual connection with yourself and the universe.

Though it is a sleeping state, your mind obtains profound creativity and vivid visualizations. You attain inspiration. This is the reason why your dreams seem so real as if you are experiencing them.

The boundary of Alpha-theta is attained at 7 to 8 Hz. This is a perfect state to program your mind, utilize maximum creative power and making conscious visualized changes in your mind. But none of this action puts any stress on your mind like the Beta waves. Your body stays relaxed.

4. Delta waves - for deep sleep at 0.5 to 4 Hz

Delta waves are the slowest brain waves that allow you to stay in deep sleep. No dreams occur during this stage of sleep. You reach the maximum depths of meditative states and lose all sense of awareness.

Delta waves take your brain to its unconscious level. Your brain obtains the access to the unconsciously present information, but you do not feel aware of it.

This state of mind is essential to heal and regenerate. Your mind and body go through a healing process during this state of sleep.

5. Gamma waves - insight wave beyond 40 Hz

The most recent discovery in the field of brain waves is the gamma waves. The research works are at their initial stages, but gamma waves are believed to be associated with exceptional processing of information and incredible insight.

So, it seems clear that you need to achieve Alpha waves to increase your capacity to learn. However, if you want to memorize things, Theta waves can help along with the Gamma waves, as they offer IQ increase and exceptional cognitive functionality.

When you ask- **When can I learn it at my full potential?**

It depends on the type of learning you want. Is it memorizing formulas, facts, and information? Or, is it about learning a skill or a process?

Learning a skill or a process is best possible if you reach the Alpha state of mind.

Therefore, the next logical question is - how can you get to the Alpha state of brain waves?

Alpha is the only state in which you feel extremely relaxed and stay awake at the same time. The alpha waves are the reasons your brain feels relaxed. Nevertheless, triggering that state requires some effort.

It is important to attain this state if you want to learn something. Without a relaxed mental state, your mind feels worried and stressed about things that actually do not matter.

Here is how you can reach trigger alpha waves in your brain:

1. Let your body and mind relax

Sounds simple, but it takes a lot of effort to relax your body and mind.

First and foremost, you need to choose a suitable time — no need to rush things or worry about everything around you. So, pick a time when you can focus on relaxing your body and mind. If you feel worried about something, write it down and put it in a box. This technique will help your mind focus on the relaxation.

Getting comfortable is another factor you should care about. A comfortable place where you can lie down would be perfect. You can sit as well, but lying down helps in achieving the alpha state faster. However, the comfort level is important. In addition, make sure you do not fall asleep.

After getting a comfortable space, you can get rid of the environmental distractions. So, switch off your mobile phone, close the doors, windows and your eyes. Even remove the clock to avoid hearing its repetitive sound. However, you can listen to slow, soothing music if you feel like.

Now, you can start removing all the clutters from your mind. The thoughts will keep running, so do not fight them. Follow a gradual approach and look at those thoughts from an observational point of view. At the same time, increase your concentration on the surrounding silence or on the tune of the music you are listening to. Eventually, your thoughts will start fading away.

2. Manage your deep breathing

Slow and deep breathing is an important approach to reaching the alpha state. Ideally, you can inhale a deep breath via your nose and exhale slowly via your mouth. You can also choose only one pathway to inhale and exhale air. But make sure you keep the pace slow.

To take deep breaths, you can focus on breathing via the diaphragm. The diaphragm is located a little below the chest area; you need to focus there when breathing. You can start the process by putting one hand in the middle of your chest and one hand on the diaphragm area. Then, breathe by moving mostly the hand you have put on the diaphragm area.

Increasing deep breathing is not necessarily possible at once. So, you can try mixing deep breaths with normal breaths initially. Try taking a normal breath after every deep breath. Eventually keep increasing the numbers of deep breaths and reduce normal breathing.

Many people find it easier to attain deep breathing by counting. The process involves counting 1-7, as you inhale air. Then, you can count 1-8, as you exhale. This way, you can monitor your breathing, make it slow, and even.

Small deep breathing sessions with tiny breaks can also help. You can set a timer and manage your breathing for 9 to 10 minutes. Then, stop for 5 minutes and begin the process again. In two to four attempts, you can reach the desired deep breathing level.

3. Visualize yourself in a peaceful place

After relaxing and attaining deep breathing, you can take yourself to a peaceful place. This is like daydreaming. The imaginary place in your head should be peaceful.

For example, you can imagine yourself in a small cottage amidst green hills. Keep your eyes closed and start walking towards the mountain from the cottage. You are still not there in the right state of mind. This is just the construction process. You can include your senses by looking at the details of the sight you are imagining. Try touching leaves, listening to the sound of falling water and smelling the moisture. Eventually, you will reach the alpha state.

Now, that you know how to attain the right mental state to learn efficiently, it is time to learn some mnemonics.

Mnemonics are methods utilized for accelerated learning and memory improvement. The term 'mnemonic' has come from Greek culture. Anciently, there was a goddess named Mnemosyne in Greek culture. She was known as the goddess who grants memory. The modern mnemonic techniques have been derived from there. Hence, mnemonics are techniques used for brain training to enhance memory.

When it comes to memorizing difficult stuff, mnemonics become a great strategy. This includes using rhymes, acronyms, association approach and plenty of techniques to utilize your visual, verbal and other kinds of memory sensitivities.

With the right mnemonics, you can easily memorize the following stuff:

- A long presentation
- Vocabulary
- Facts
- Speeches
- Phone numbers
- Ideas
- Faces and names

- Numbers

And more!

Whenever you want to learn something new, your limited memory becomes a hurdle. That is when mnemonics come into play, allowing you accelerated learning with certain patterns. These strategies do require some practice initially, but once you master them, they take your memory to a whole new level of excellence. You obtain an organized and well-coordinated network of information in your brain. This way, remembering becomes an easy job for you.

Chapter 4 – Visual Mnemonics: Tools & Techniques

The most effective mnemonic strategies include visual imagery. From making lists to developing links and memory palaces – you can use your visual memory and learn faster in plenty of ways.

Here are some great visual techniques you can leverage:

The Journey Method

Given in the popular book **How to Develop a Perfect Memory** by Dominic O'Brien, the Journey Method is quite effective in memorizing through journeys and places.

In the Journey Method, you use familiar places as anchors for things you want to remember. Then, these anchors are arranged in a serial order to create a journey of memories. For example, you can utilize your classroom, office, or room to develop a mental visualized journey of memories.

This method works effectively because of the familiarity of the places you use as anchors. So, no need to say that you need to pick highly familiar journeys. For example, you can choose your route to office or college as a journey for memory.

Here is how it works-

Suppose you want to memorize the whole periodic table for a college presentation. So, you will need some anchors for the elements in each group.

1. Start by making a list of all the interesting things available

in your room. This can include your desk, laptop, bookshelf, bin, drawer, and others. Make sure you choose distinguishable objects.

2. Now, divide that list in a clockwise order. So, scan from the left and reach the right side to memorize the sequence of every object you have selected.

3. In your mind, put elements of the first group in the first object from the left. So, H, Li, Na, K, Rb, Cs, and Fr can go on the desk.

4. Put the elements of the next group in the next object available in the sequence present in your room. Hence, Be, Mg, Ca, Sr, Ba, and Ra can go in your laptop.

5. Do the same thing in a sequence from left to right.

6. Eventually, you will create a memorable anchor for elements in every group.

7. Visualize this until you become confident about the memory.

Effective use of this technique requires deciding your anchors and journey in advance. The sequence of the landmarks should be clear in your head. Then, you can easily link them with information and make memorable associations. Choose the most memorable landmarks when creating a mental journey.

This approach can help you memorize events, experiments, people, objects and other elements.

For example, if you want to memorize the sequence of a presentation at work, you can use this method.

1. Select your office building as your mental journey.

2. From entering the office building to reaching the conference room, decide the required number of anchors. So, you can pick the entry gate, reception, lift, main office, your office, and conference room.

3. Now, make a list of presentation sequence you want to follow and include in the mental journey.

4. At the entry gate - welcoming everyone present during the presentation.

5. At the reception - introducing the purpose of the presentation.

6. Lift - going through every step of concepts of that presentation.

7. Main office - describing the importance of the presented information for your company.

8. Your office - explaining your personal views on the idea presented.

9. Conference room - closing with an overview and thanking everyone.

That is it! You will remember the whole presentation without even using your fingertips. Your mental journey, from the office entry to the conference room, will let you go through every aspect of your presentation step-by-step.

The method is flexible, so you can easily change the anchors and information, as per your requirements. However, it is important to follow a sequence when deciding these. That is the whole point of the Journey Method.

Linking

Linking is another tool you can use to memorize lists of objects, places and other types of information in a fixed sequence.

This method involves a fun process of using your creativity in making mental imagery for items on a list and creating a memorable sequence.

Let's find out how it works-

Suppose you have to memorize a list of items in the same order. You can write those elements in the fixed order and assign every element to a mental image.

For example, let's consider that your list contains the following items:

- Firefighter
- Chef
- Apple pie
- Pirate
- Cowboy
- Soldier
- Pizza
- Trouser
- Spider

You can memorize it by using the following linking approach:

1. Pick one image for every item in the list. So, your

firefighter can be sitting on a couch watching TV.

2. Link every image with the other somehow. For instance, the FIREFIGHTER, sitting on a couch watching master CHEF on TV.

3. Go through this mental sequence 2-3 times to memorize.

And there you have it! You can use this linking approach to remember any list, no matter how long it is. Dominic O'Brien also gives this great method in his book **How to Develop a Perfect Memory**.

This method is effective because of the visualized and emotional approach it utilizes. You already know that our brain is wired to respond quickly to visual cues and emotional cues. Hence, the creative freedom of picking your mental scenarios allows you to retain the created links in the correct sequence.

But there's a catch here! This method works only if you give yourself complete creative freedom when creating mental pictures. To do so:

- Do not change the first image that comes to your mind. The first image is the image that stays permanently.

- Stop judging yourself if an image is weird or strange. We are human with a complex mind, so embrace it.

- Try associating a strong emotion with your images such as surprise, excitement, shock or any other.

- Associate with a moving image such as fighting, swimming, dancing, running or any other.

Keeping the given tips in mind, you can make this linking method extremely effective for your memory improvement. With practice, you become better at this, and your mental images become brighter and clearer. Therefore, you can begin accelerated learning with this approach.

For exams' preparation:

Students find revision process hectic before exams especially if your exam syllabus is huge with many chapters.

In that case, you would want to utilize the linking method to memorize concepts in the right sequence.

Suppose you have to memorize a diagram, which contains the following elements in a sequence:

- Two men
- One girl
- Four tall buildings
- Three small houses
- A garden
- Five trees
- One main road
- Six interconnected streets

To memorize this diagram in the same sequence, you can follow the linking method:

1. Two men - fighting with each other.
2. One girl - shouting to call the police.
3. Four tall buildings - giving shadows to the fighting men.
4. Three small houses - where policemen are standing.

5. A garden - where two men are fighting.

6. Five trees - shredding leaves slowly.

7. One main road - many cars honking loudly.

8. Six interconnected streets - bulls chasing people.

If you observe, all the imaginary scenarios contain strong imagery and have connections with each other. You have to do the same to make every item a strong memory. Then, go through it once by visualizing. If you forget one or more items, try modifying their images in your mind. Follow the same process until you memorize the whole sequence.

Initially, it can seem complicated, but practice will give you necessary brain training for faster learning.

At work:

Linking is not limited to students preparing their exams, even managers and knowledge workers can utilize this approach at work.

What if you have to pitch a product to a client? Your boss has put his faith in you, so you cannot miss any detail or look nervous when presenting that product.

In that case, you have to make a clear sequence of every element associated with that product. Only then, you can confidently present the product and convince your client to buy.

Suppose your product involves the following specifications in a sequence:

- Beautiful design
- Affordable price

- Durable body
- Low maintenance
- Customer support
- Warranty

This is quite a small list, but you can utilize linking for long lists of items too. The process is the same as mentioned before. You have to associate each item with an image in your mind and visual it all in a sequence.

So:

1. **Beautiful design** - a BEAUTIFUL girl dancing slowly, wearing a golden dress.

2. **Affordable price** - the golden dress looks dull and CHEAP.

3. **Durable body** - the dancing girl suddenly starts doing PUSHUPS.

4. **Low maintenance** - the music stops, so a mechanic comes and picks up the equipment.

5. **Customer support** - the dancing girl, is talking to the mechanic.

6. **Warranty** - the mechanic is fixing the sound equipment right there on the dance floor.

With similar mental images, you can create a sequence of actions to memorize a difficult list of things when working.

Learning words in a foreign language:

Known as an expert of practical use of mnemonics, Dr. Michael

Gruneberg has derived this approach called Linkword. His techniques are similar to the linking approach, which help in learning words from German, French, Italian and Spanish languages.

His Linkword books include clear mental pictures, which readers can use to learn foreign languages. Hundreds of words are divided into small groups of ten words in each group. Every group is some category, which allows you to make sense of each.

Then, you get clear imagery ideas of linking words with mental pictures. For example, to remember "Hummer," you are advised to picture a funny lobster because Hummer means lobster in German. Similarly, there are unique examples of imaginary visuals for hundreds of words to visualize and learn foreign languages faster.

The Memory Palace

The memory palace is a modern version of the Journey Method given by Dominic O'Brien. However, it has been famous since the ancient Roman era with the name Method of Loci.

A new version is appreciated because it has more fun elements attached, which makes this version effective for many people.

To remember a list of information, you choose a familiar place instead of a journey. For example, you can choose your home, your office, your kid's room or any other place you are familiar with. Then, you create a crazy story involving that place and the elements of the list you want to memorize.

So, if your list has items:

- Oranges

- Apple juice
- Paper cups

You can imagine your kid's room and create a memory palace like this:

1. You enter the room, and your kid is juggling four oranges at once.//
2. The floor is filled with apple juice.
3. Hundreds of paper cups are visible in the pool of apple juice.

Sure, this is a small exercise, but it can go to any length depending on the size of the list you have.

5 Steps to Successfully Create and Utilize the Memory Palace

1. Create your palace

The most important part of this technique is the place you pick in your mind. The palace should be visible in your mind. So, choose a place you are most familiar with. You should be able to visit every corner of that place in your mind. That is why picking your own house seems the best option. You know your home in detail, so the memorizing part becomes easier.

After picking a place, you need to think about the route you want to take when you are visualizing it. A route is better than looking at a static image. You can start walking from room to room and recall things that you remember in every room.

Here are more examples you can use to create a memory palace:

- Pick a street you are most familiar with and follow a sequence you generally follow. So, driving to your workplace, walking to the supermarket and other rides can become a memory palace.

- We all remember our former schools so that they can become a great choice of memory palace. You can even pick your current institution and use classrooms, the library, and other elements to make a route in your mind.

- How about the indoors of your office. You know every corner there, so make your office cubicle, conference room, and other places a part of your memory palace.

- For more soothing scenarios, you can imagine yourself jogging in a green surrounding where you frequently go.

2. *Figure out distinctive features*

Choosing a palace in your mind does the first job only. You have to enhance its clarity and detailing in your mind. For that purpose, it is important that you go through the palace mentally repeatedly to pick distinctive features.

Start by closing your eyes and noticing the first thing you see when looking at your memory palace. Is it the color of the surface, or the front door of your home? Keep going through the mental route and analyze everything you see mentally.

Make sure you choose a fixed process when analyzing your memory palace. For instance, if you look left and move to the right, do that every time you are in your memory palace. The same thing is required with the turns you take and the elements you seek in a sequence.

Keep creating a mental note of every element that you see. This will enhance the visibility of your memory palace through your mental eyes.

3. Practice visualizing the palace repeatedly

The Memory Palace technique can only work if the elements are imprinted perfectly. So, practicing is key here. If you are already sensitive to visual thinking, this process will not seem difficult. Otherwise, you can:

- Go to the place, follow the same route physically, and keep saying every feature you see.

- Make a list of every feature you see in the selected route, then, follow the same route in your mind to find all those features. Even now, you can say the names of the features you see.

- Follow your point view every time you are mentally walking through the memory palace.

- When you think you are ready, do it once again to be sure about the features of the route.

4. Assign memories

Now that you have a clear memory palace with distinctive features, you can assign those features with memories and memorize them. The assigning process is the same as the Journey Method. You can be as strange as possible; it all depends on how easily you can remember that mental picture.

5. Repeat and repeat!

After the first four steps, you become ready to memorize things using your memory palace. However, the technique is still new to you, so it would be better if you constantly repeat and practice. Do not just go to the memory palace only when you want to memorize something. Keep using the mental route and see if the assigned memories come on their own as soon as you see the associated features.

Stay relaxed during the whole process, and you can successfully create and utilize the memory palace technique.

Association or Memory Pegging

When you attach a memory to a mental visual, it is called a memory peg, and the process is known as memory pegging or association. This method, however, is more effective when you want to memorize abstract items such as concepts, numbers, names, and words. Everything that does not hold an emotional value to us. This method has also been given in the book **How to Develop a Perfect Memory** by Dominic O'Brien.

You take abstract items and associate them with things that matter to you such as objects, locations or people.

Here is **how it works**:

1. You allow your mind to soak abstract information for a while.

2. Calm yourself down to reach a relaxed state.

3. You ask yourself - what do I remember when I say this information?

4. You create a chain of mental images, which leads to a vivid memory of that abstract information.

The process requires truthfulness and absence of resistance. You need to be genuine with the images that come to your mind. Do not hold back. You can be ridiculous, crazy, extraordinary, unusual, animated or anything else — no need to judge yourself or try to stop from controlling the trail of thoughts. Just go with the flow and see where it takes you. The first instincts will give you the best memories to retain the knowledge. That is an essential key to memory improvement.

And remember, if it seems boring, you're doing it all wrong!

Association method works because you allow your brain to flow freely. Abstract ideas are difficult for our brain to store because they stay disconnected from our important memories. For example, a student does not feel any emotional attachment to a mathematical formula, but he does feel happy when playing a video game. So, associating the formula with that video game can help. The brain can create a permanent memory network and bring the memory back through the same route.

If a student wants to use association for brain training, he or she can do this for example:

You want to memorize the word "Strenuous," which means "difficult."

1. "Strenuous."

2. I am thinking "Strength."

3. Strength reminds me of the "Hulk."

4. Handling the Hulk is pretty difficult for others in the movie Avengers.

5. Hulk is STRENGTH; Hulk is DIFFICULT.

Students can use this technique to associate abstract information with things that hold importance in their brain. This way, exam preparation can become way easier than usual.

Even professionals can utilize this process to make their work easier. For instance:

You want to remember the name of every client who would be present in a meeting.

1. "Ryan."

2. I can think of a party where I saw a kid "Ryan." He was holding a big lollipop.

3. This gives a picture of the client "Ryan" holding a lollipop in his mouth.

As mentioned before, you can be as ridiculous as your mind allows you to be — no need to restrict your mental images.

Association is pretty much a combination of linking approach and the Journey Method. You can link an abstract idea with a more memorable one. Or, you can create an imaginary, but familiar scenario. Nevertheless, there's a catch. You can't choose associations given by other people as your own. Of course, sometimes it works, but mostly it does not help you create a long-term memory. The association has to be your creation, so that it automatically creates a memory network in your brain. Your connection matters.

The Dominic System

Another great visualization exercise for brain training from Dominic O'Brien. In his book **How to Develop a Perfect Memory**, he has explained his Dominic System to provide ready-made links of associated memories to memorize large numbers.

This system is great for students and professionals who have to memorize large numbers on a daily basis.

Here is **how it works**:

An abstract idea is associated with a person, an action or an object, which is known as the **PAO System**.

1. You take single digits from 0 to 9 and associate them with single alphabets A, B, C, D, E and so on.

2. 0 becomes A, 1, becomes B, and so on.

3. Now, digit pairs from 00 to 99 are replaced with letter pairs, using a significant association.

This will create a ready-to-use system for you to remember any number, no matter how large it is.

The process works better and better as you practice it. Regular use allows you to remember the associated letter with every digit. So, you can create real-time visuals in your brain and memorize large numbers faster.

For students, this method is exceptionally effective due to the presence of numbers in all major subjects such as mathematics, physics, chemistry, and others. Even topics such as history and geography require number memory. In history, you are supposed to memorize exact years of events. In geography, you have to memorize coordinates along with the name of places.

Here is how it can work for you:

You want to memorize the year 1954 of the Civil Rights Movement.

- 19 = BJ = **B**ig **J**am/ all over the city.

- 54 = FE = **F**lying **E**agle/ in the sky.

Similarly, you can memorize larger numbers using the same method. Just use the letters and create your associations using the same process.

For people at work, this method can make data analysis and its use more convenient. When you are good with numbers, people take you more seriously. So, using this method seems effective for knowledge workers and managers too.

Suppose, you want to memorize a sales data which includes a large number. Then, you can use the same method and create useful associations to memorize that number. Similarly, you can memorize multiple passwords, security codes, and other valuable numbers.

For instance, you want to memorize your computer password, which is 2569.

25 = CF = **C**at **F**lying/ in a balloon.

69 = GJ = **G**o **J**oker/ find Batman.

When you have an odd number, pairing all of them is not possible. Do not worry! There is a solution for that as well:

1. You can divide digits 1-9 and turn each one of them into objects.
2. 1 becomes a candle, 2 becomes a swan and so on.
3. Make zero a football.

Done! You have all the numbers associated with objects that look like those numbers. The shape of the object is critical here. It should remind you of the number you are associating it with.

So, now, you have both versions of the Dominic System. Make sure you practice them frequently to become better with time.

Reviewing

Dominic O'Brien has another book called **You Can Have an Amazing Memory**. In this, he explains the use of reviewing in creating long-term memories of important things.

The process is simple:

1. You come across any information.

2. Review that information once, and then leave it for a while.

3. Then, you review that information 5 times at intervals of 48 hours, 7 days, 30 days, and then, 3 months.

The purpose of distributed reviewing is to allow your brain to refresh that memory repeatedly until the neural network becomes permanent. Therefore, this approach is more about patiently following the process and letting your mind soak every detail of the information.

The keys to successfully using this method are:

1. Giving yourself the proper time to visit your mental route when reviewing.

2. Stopping at every route station and letting the details sink in.

3. Finding weak links and working on them every time you review.

So, there you have it! All the visual mnemonics to help you in accelerated learning. Now, you can reach the level of photographic memory.

Chapter 5 – Verbal Mnemonics: Tools & Techniques

You can also leverage your auditory sensitivity to memorize stuff with following tools and techniques.

Coding mnemonics

To remember difficult numbers, you can utilize the sense of sound too. The numbers such as security numbers, contact numbers, important dates, and others can become impossible for some people to remember generally.

Imagine you talked for hours to a potential client and gotten his number. But the next moment, you cannot even remember a single digit. Such situations can occur and become painful in every professional's life. Similarly, students lose important marks in test papers just because of one silly mistake of adding a wrong date or a year.

But numbers are easier to remember if you focus on the sound they make when you say them out loud.

For example:

- 0 = z, s or c (0 sounds to start with z, s, or c)
- 1 = w or v
- 2 = t, u, o (u and o because it ends with a sound of u or o)
- 3 = th

- 4 = f, ph,
- 5 = fy, phl
- 6 = sh, ch
- 7 = ss, sey
- 8 = I, ay
- 9 = n

That is how you get the sound of each digit from 0 to 9. Then, you can choose relevant words using the same sounds and associate them with the numbers.

For students, this coding method can help in memorizing geographical facts, mathematical formulas, historical dates and more. Similarly, **knowledge workers** can use this method to learn passwords, security numbers, or important data while preparing for a meeting or presentation.

For example, if you want to learn:

1. Amazon is 3990 miles long.
2. The Nile is 4140 miles long.

You can utilize the coding mnemonics like this:

1. Amazon- 3990 = th-n-n-s = Thanos nose
2. Nile- 4140 = f-v-f-s = favorite fist

It does not have to be meaningful. If it makes sense to you, then, you can memorize the numbers. Focus on the sounds of the numbers. That is most important in this technique.

Acronyms or Chunking

Chunking is a process you can use to group items, information, and ideas in an organized manner. The purpose is to make things easier to remember. The same process is utilized in creating acronyms.

Acronym process allows you to make your own words using the initial letter or initial two letters of every word you want to remember.

For example, the combination of colors present in sunlight is called VIBGYOR:

Violet

Indigo

Blue

Green

Yellow

Orange

Red

So, you can create your acronyms whenever you have a big list of words to memorize.

Acrostics

When you want to remember words in a particular order, the acrostic approach works as well. You can create a sentence in which every word will start with a letter representing the word you want to remember.

For example, if you want to memorize the seven continents:

1. North America
2. South America
3. Antarctica
4. Europe
5. Asia
6. Africa
7. Australia

You can make a sentence using the first letter of each continent's name.

So, it can be:

Never **s**ound **a**dult, **e**ven **as** **a**n **a**dult.

Each first letter here is representing the beginning of each continent's name. You can do the same with other groups of words you want to memorize. If you want to memorize certain abstract words associated with your business presentation, this method can help. The process is fun and stays on your mind.

Rhyming

Rhyming is about arranging words in such an order that words with similar sounds get equidistant places. The meaning of the sentence changes, but the sound and the words help you remember better. Then, you can rearrange to the original order after memorizing it.

Here are a few examples:

If you want to memorize - Columbus started his sail in 1492.

This sentence has a popular rhyming form - **In 1492,**

Columbus sailed the ocean blue.

You can create your rhymes to remember information if it suits you.

Chapter 6 – Food for Your Memory

Until now, you have understood how complex your brain functionality is. The process of developing neural networks is a consistent task, which your brain does.

If your brain keeps on performing, you can memorize anything and create long-term retrievable memories. However, that is possible only if you keep having required nutrients.

Just like your body muscles, your brain also requires nutrition to stay healthy and work at maximum capacity.

There are specific nutrients that come from specific food and beverages. This chapter will give you a complete understanding of how certain food and beverages affect positively on your brain's function and memory.

1. *Fatty fish*

No other food can top the nutritional value offered by fatty fish to the brain.

Such fish types include sardines, trout, and salmon. They all contain omega-3 fatty acids, which is highly beneficial for brain and memory power.

Our brain contains about 60 percent of fat, and about 50 percent of brain fat is omega-3. This type of fat is utilized to create nerve cells and brain cells. At the same time, this fat assists in memory creation and learning.

You already know that learning new skills is about developing neural networks and strengthening them consistently. The process becomes easier when your brain receives an optimum amount of fatty acid.

There are plenty of other benefits your brain attains with fatty fish foods.

One of them is the slow decline of mental capacity as you age. This is also because of the nerve cells and memory construction generated with the help of an omega-3 type of fat.

You can include fatty fish in your diet in broiled or baked form to obtain the maximum quantity of omega-3 fat. This will promote gray matter in your brain, which includes nerve cells of the memory, emotions, and decision capacity.

2. *Coffee*

If you are a coffee drinker, you can feel glad because it is beneficial for your brain.

Coffee contains two kinds of components that help your brain - Antioxidants and caffeine.

A controlled quantity of caffeine in your body provides a temporary boost to your brain power. This component is known to block adenosine in your brain, which causes sleepiness. Hence, you feel alert and awake.

At the same time, caffeine triggers serotonin and other neurotransmitters that make you feel happy. This way, you can improve your mood and feel positive. And a positive attitude is a must in accelerated learning. So, you can understand the importance!

According to studies conducted on caffeine, researchers have found that it enhances concentration. Concentration is a must-have trait for students, managers and knowledge workers.

3. Dark-colored berries such as blueberries

Among plenty of health benefits, dark-colored berries usually contain anthocyanins. This compound stays available in blueberries as well and offers antioxidant and anti-inflammatory effects.

Oxidative stress is one of the common reasons why our brain loses its capacity with time. This type of stress triggers the degeneration of neuron networks. With age, this problem causes low memory efficiency. In the worst-case scenario, an oxidative state can turn into neurodegenerative diseases as well.

Having enough blueberries and other dark-colored berries can help you have an ample amount of antioxidants. They work to control oxidative stress along with the restriction of inflammation.

The antioxidants of blueberries reach your brain and help in brain cell communication. This component is accumulated between the brain cells, which provides a comfortable path for brain cells to communicate with each other.

You can include blueberries in your cereal every day. Or, make smoothies with some blueberries to gain antioxidants.

4. Turmeric

Turmeric is a spice that looks yellow. Usually available in curry powder, this spice is a major source of curcumin.

Curcumin holds the capacity to reach your brain cells easily and provide anti-inflammatory and antioxidant benefits.

This compound allows your brain to have a strong memory. The signs of depression go away when this compound triggers dopamine and serotonin in your brain.

Regular use of turmeric in your food provides enough curcumin to enhance the neurotrophic factor of your brain. This factor is responsible for the growth of brain cells. This is an important brain health benefit because our brain cells start dying as we age.

You can include turmeric in the spices prepared for veggies and meat dishes. Some people also like to make turmeric tea to gain curcumin.

5. Broccoli

Broccoli contains vitamin K, antioxidants and plenty of other plant-based compounds. Vitamin K is fat-soluble, which has an important job in our brain. The brain utilizes this vitamin to create sphingolipids, which is another kind of fat required for healthy brain cells. This way, broccoli can enhance your brainpower and memory.

Along with vitamin K, you get antioxidants that further support your memory and brain performance. With just 1 cup of broccoli every day, you can obtain the require RDI or Recommended Daily Intake.

6. Pumpkin seeds

Some valuable elements become available to your brain with regular intake of pumpkin seeds. These elements include zinc, magnesium, copper, and iron. Every element has its purpose regarding brain health and memory power.

With Zinc, your brain strengthens its nerve signals. Hence, the connection between neurons stays strong. Plus, regular intake of pumpkin seeds allows you to enhance your learning process. The new neuron networks form faster, so you learn faster.

Magnesium is another beneficial element that enhances your memory and learning capacity. It keeps your brain protected from neurological diseases, migraines, epilepsy, and depression as well.

Pumpkin seeds are also a great source of copper that increases the capacity of sending nerve signals. The optimum amount of copper helps nerve networks to work efficiently and create memories that last for long periods.

Iron is also a necessary requirement to keep your brain function in top-notch condition.

All these micronutrients are available in pumpkin seeds. So, you can give yourself a lot of brain power by adding this ingredient to your meals.

7. Dark chocolate

You can enjoy dark chocolate and drinks made with cocoa powder to obtain plenty of brain-boosting nutrients such as antioxidants, flavonoids, and caffeine.

Flavonoids are a combination of multiple antioxidant compounds that come from the plant. The flavonoids obtained from chocolate reach brain areas where memories and learnings are stored. The neural networks get stronger quickly with dark chocolate's flavonoids, which helps in accelerated learning.

Along with memory strength, dark chocolate also affects mood by driving positive feelings.

8. Nuts

Nuts and brain health are associated and backed by various studies. Nuts usually contain antioxidants, healthy fats as well as vitamin E. All three nutrients are directly related to our brain health. Vitamin E increases the strength of cell membranes in our brain. Hence, the brain becomes protected from free radicals that are known to decline memory power.

Among all kinds of nuts, walnuts come on top when it comes to brain health. Walnut contains omega-3 fatty acids. And you already know this fatty acid improves brain's health and memory power.

9. Oranges

Do you like orange juice? If yes, then you are gaining an important nutrient for your brain.

Oranges and all other tangy fruits include vitamin C, which is an antioxidant. It fights against the brain free radicals that attack brain cells. Hence, your mental power stays strong for a long time.

Other sources of vitamin C include kiwi, guava, tomatoes, bell peppers and strawberries as well. You can make smoothies, salads or have a glass of juice to gain enough vitamin C for your brain.

10. Eggs

With eggs, you gain folate, choline, vitamin B6 and vitamin B12. And they are all associated with brain health.

Enough quantity of choline promotes the creation of

acetylcholine, which works as a neurotransmitter. This neurotransmitter ensures your relaxed mood and allows your mind to remember things accurately. High intake of choline is a necessity to increase your memory power. However, most people do not get enough.

Egg yolks contain high choline content to help you gain the benefits. With one egg yolk, you get about 112 mg of choline. Men need to have about 550 mg of choline every day. On the other hand, women require about 425 mg every day. With that, you can decide the number of eggs in your daily diet.

Eggs will also give you vitamin B6 and vitamin B12. These vitamins keep your brain away from depressing thoughts and increase memory holding capacity. B12 has a special power of controlling sugar content in your brain.

11. *Green tea*

Green tea is a healthier alternative to coffee to have ample caffeine in your brain. The benefits are similar such as brain performance, focus, alertness, and the ability to increase memory.

Along with the caffeine, green tea also provides L-theanine, which is a type of amino acid. This amino acid works on improving the activity of GABA neurotransmitter, which allows the brain to feel relaxed. Hence, green tea is advised when you want to attain a light meditative state by promoting alpha brain waves. You can concentrate better and improve your creativity levels without going to sleep.

You can also use green tea for antioxidants and polyphenols that help the brain stay protected from neurodegeneration.

12. Avocados

Avocados are also a great source of brain fats, folate, and vitamin K. These components working together protect from blood clotting in your brain. Cognitive functionality stays top-notch, which assists in concentrating and building long-term memories.

Along with vitamin K, avocados also contain vitamin B and C. Their low sugar and high protein contents are one of the rare nutrient combinations you find in fruits.

You can make smoothies with avocados, include them in baked dishes, and other forms to enjoy the taste and improve brain health.

13. Beets

A not so favorite of many, but beets score top marks when it comes to brain health and performance. The presence of natural nitrates in beets helps in keeping a steady flow of blood in the brain. Hence, your brain functionality enhances, which allows you to stay alert and feel focused.

14. Bone Broth

Bone broth has been known to improve brain health since ancient times. The broth included in your recipes allow your body to obtain various amino acids such as glycine and proline. These amino acids increase the immune system and memory building capacity.

15. Bananas

As you already know, potassium promotes the generation of

brain fats. And bananas are a perfect source to obtain high potassium content on a daily basis. You can make delicious banana smoothies and give your brain enough potassium to work on nerves, brain cells and the heart as well.

16. *Spinach*

Spinach contains high quantities of nutrients such as folate, beta-carotene, and lutein. All these components are known to work on brain function and prevent dementia. Regular inclusion of spinach helps in boosting concentration.

You can have 2 cups every day in the form of salad, juice or any other form. Many people use sweet fruits with spinach to make delicious salads.

How Sugar Impacts Your Brain

Being the control room of your body, your brain requires a lot of energy. So, the availability of an optimum quantity of glucose is necessary for humans. Glucose works as a fuel to run all the activities in the brain. But just like a vehicle, there's always a limitation on the quantity of fuel you can have. High sugar content in your diet can lead to negative impacts.

Understand this - a small amount of sugar stimulates your brain to ask for more. So, when your brain asks you to have more sugar, you lose self-control and keep eating more and more sugary food. And that increased quantity reduces your cognitive skills. Sugar gives a sense of reward by stimulating the associated section in your brain. That is why your brain craves for more and more sugar to keep having that feeling.

According to dietary science experts, food types such as fatty, salty and sugary can make people addicted. This addiction can lead to overeating, loss of cognitive control and increased weight. Plus, thinking about eating all the time does not allow your brain to think about other valuable stuff such as learning or memory training.

It all started to keep early humans alive with a calorie-rich diet. The stimulus helped in selecting high-calorie food, which helped in the survival of early humans. However, the scenarios have changed now, and the same stimulus is making people diabetic, obese and reducing brain functionality.

Increased sugar in your body holds the capacity to damage blood vessels. That damage impacts your heart and brain as well. In the brain, vessels associated with your ability to see can get damaged. If you get diabetic, your brain cells lose their performance progressively. So, your ability to learn goes down, motor speed reduces, and memory building capacity decreases as well.

Eating high sugary food regularly can lead to diminishing mental capacity. It increases the HbA1c levels in your brain, which causes brain shrinkage. This is possible even if you do not get diabetes. Anyone who has a high consumption of sugar every day can say goodbye to optimum cognitive function. Other associated impacts involve hypertension, hyperglycemia, insulin resistance, and enhanced cholesterol levels. In addition, it all reduces your overall brain health.

So, the ultimate question is - how do you save your brain from sugar?

You cannot stop sugar intake completely. But, you can choose better versions of sugar. For instance, using refined sugar or food with added sugar are bad choices for your brain's health. You can satisfy your need for sugar with fresh fruits. You cannot even choose too much honey, agave or maple syrup, as they all contain concentrated sugar content.

Chapter 7 – Physical Fitness for Improved Memory and Brain Function

Your brain is connected to your body. So, if your body is in its peak condition, your brain does not have to put too much pressure on various functions. Your physical health directly impacts your brain function and increases your ability to concentrate and hold memories.

Sitting all day trying to solve a problem is not the best way to sharpen your learning skills. You need to combine it with good physical exercises to improve brain training and information processing.

Let us understand the science behind physical fitness and its connection to your brain's health.

You know that your heart rate increases when you indulge in a physical workout. That increased heart rate allows more oxygen to reach blood cells, which reaches every body part including your brain. More oxygen in your brain assists in triggering healthy hormones. As a result, all the existing brain cells perform at a higher rate and new neural networks are developed at the same time.

Experts call it brain plasticity, which is the growth of neural networks in your brain. Working out stimulates the process of brain plasticity. Various cortical areas obtain new connections between brain cells, which improve memory power, concentration, and overall brain function.

With exercise, you can experience these changes occurring in your brain. Refreshed happy mood instead of depressing thoughts, better focus and many other benefits help you live and learn effectively. Moreover, your brain can effectively fight insulin resistance, inflammation, and other degenerative factors. The chemical condition in your brain stays balanced, which helps in the long-term survival of neural networks and brain cells.

Here are all the brain health advantages you can expect from physical exercise:

1. *Stress reduction*

A hectic day at work, or the pressure of an upcoming exam. You can release your stress with a good workout session. Walk, jog, or head to the gym for some weightlifting. All kinds of exercises release feel-good hormones in your brain, allowing you to think positive thoughts and feel refreshed. A component called norepinephrine increases in your brain when you exercise. This component balances the stress, allowing you to get a better perspective of things. So, you can refresh yourself with a good workout and get ready for another round of working at the office or preparing for your exam.

2. *Increased happiness*

People, who exercise feel happier than the people who do not. And happiness is associated with a healthy mental state, which lets you focus and promotes accelerated learning. Exercise triggers the release of endorphins in your brain. Using this hormone, your brain gives you feelings such as euphoria and happiness.

Regular exposure to stress can lead to depression. However,

exercise keeps on balancing it with endorphins. Hence, your mind feels elevated above anxiety and depression. You do not have to spend hours lifting a weight. Simply 20 to 30 minutes of regular exercise can give you protection from anxiety, depression, and stress.

3. Confident personality

Whether you are a student, a knowledge worker or a manager, a confident personality is a necessary trait to thrive in your career. Nevertheless, you can't feel confident if your brain does not allow you to. Confidence comes from the self-esteem for your mental and physical capacities.

With regular workout, you get to see a better version of yourself both physically and mentally. In addition, that improved self-image leads to a confident personality. No matter what your body weight is, or how old you are, regular exercise lets you believe in your abilities.

A confident personality is important in life, especially if you want to learn things constantly. For students, memory improvement and learning provide better scores in exams. For professionals, learning is about reaching higher designations. You can do all that only if you have confidence in your capabilities, including appearance and mental capacity. And that is exactly what physical fitness does for you.

4. Protection from gradual cognitive decline

No one wants it, but our age decreases our ability to memorize and even think properly. In the worst-case scenario, cognitive decline reaches the level of Alzheimer's. Brain cells die, and brain functions gradually stop working.

While Alzheimer's is the extreme condition, cognitive decline is common in almost every person. People, with some knowledge of cognitive decline, think that it begins after crossing the age of 45. This is true, but you have to start worrying about it way before to protect your brain functions.

Exercising regularly prevents the degeneration of brain cells. Beginning at an early age, you can exercise to increase the healthy chemical content in your brain. Hence, your brain obtains the capacity to support the hippocampus that plays a big role in the functions of learning and memory.

5. Development of new brain cells

If you invest time in cardiovascular exercise, it is helping your brain by developing new cells. More cells mean higher brain performance. High-intensity workout enhances a type of protein in your brain, which is called BDNF. This protein is derived in your brain and improves your mental capacities. You can think faster and go to deeper levels of the thinking process. It also improves your decision-making capacity and enhances your ability to learn new things faster.

New brain cells promote the development of new memory networks in your brain. Hence, applying all the memory tools and getting results can become easier if you spend time gaining physical fitness.

The production of new brain cells majorly takes place in the hippocampus area of your brain. This happens due to the increased oxygen content that reaches your brain through the blood pumped by your heart. The new cells in your brain's hippocampus create better conditions for memory building and neural connections. Hence, learning gets easier. This increased brain cells can improve your ability to memorize vocabulary or learn new skills for the job.

6. Controlled addictive behavior

All kinds of addictions are related to your brain. An imbalance in the brain chemical leads to addiction. Regular consumption of sugary food, alcohol, tobacco and other kinds of addictive components is a major reason why a brain loses its functionality.

Exercise helps in the protection as well as the recovery from addiction. Exercise promotes the release of dopamine in your brain. Dopamine is a reward or pleasure hormone that is released due to drugs, sugary foods, alcohol, sex, and exercise. So, your brain gradually de-prioritizes addictive components and gains its sense of reward through workout sessions.

High alcohol content in your body can disrupt your sleeping habits. Not being able to sleep or wake up from the sleep prevents your brain from resting. Exercise is the solution for this too. A good workout session promotes the sense of rest, which lets you attain a sound sleep without having alcohol.

7. Attaining a relaxed mental state

As you already know, a relaxed mind is necessary to attain the alpha state of mind to learn efficiently. In addition, workout sessions in moderate intensity can help you achieve that. Sound sleep and relaxed muscles are the reasons you feel comfortable. This happens after 1 to 3 hours of working out. Regular workout sessions, however, tend to make you feel relaxed immediately when you sit after an exercise session.

8. Feeling inspired and creative

An inspired and creative mindset is how you can ace accelerated learning. These two factors are probably the most important in memory improvement. So, you have to train your brain in every possible way to feel creative and inspired. Moreover, exercising is one of those ways for sure.

Workout sessions create a sync between your mind and body. You get better control over how your body and mind feel. Furthermore, a well-synced mind leads to inspirations and creativity.

The Golden Combination of Physical and Mental Exercise

To maximize brain training, you can choose physical exercises that target brain function. Though all activities are beneficial for your brainpower, some forms such as ballroom or ballet dancing require more mental involvement. Similarly, it is better to cycle than run to involve more cognitive functions in your workout sessions. Therefore, the goal should be choosing workout types that include the brain's sense of rhythm, coordination, and strategy.

Every aerobic exercise is beneficial for your body and mind. Aerobic exercises provide increased oxygen, making your brain cells healthier.

If you exercise first thing in the morning, before work or college, it keeps you relaxed all day long. You get a better perspective, and your decision-making capacity stays at its peak during the whole day.

The 4 Types of Workouts That Offer Brain Health

1. Cardio

Cardiovascular exercises are also known as aerobic exercises. You can choose a low-intensity workout such as dancing, or a high-intensity workout such as fast cycling. The intensity of cardio exercises stays flexible, so you can increase or decrease as per your choice.

These exercise types tend to elevate heart rate up to 50 to 80 percent of the maximum. Generally, people are advised to indulge in 30-40 minutes of low-intensity cardio 5 times every week. Or, you can indulge in high-intensity cardio for about 20 minutes or so, 3 times every week.

You can choose cardio exercises such as jogging, cycling, treadmill, dancing, or aerobic sessions. If you want to work on your physical health faster, high-intensity cardio works better. You can start with low-intensity and gradually increase to the higher levels. This is an excellent approach to improving your brain function as well.

2. Weightlifting

Weightlifting is effective in reaching peak physical levels and improving your brain function. Lifting weights increases the heart rate, enhances muscle and makes your bones stronger. While the first benefit helps your brain get sufficient oxygen, the other two give you a physical shape you desire.

Weightlifting programs differ regarding current body weight, body weight goals, age, gender, and diet. But, generally, you can rely on moderate weights and medium-intensity exercises. This way, you can save yourself from feeling exhausted and maximize the mental and physical benefits of weight training.

A great advantage with weight training is that you can focus on specific muscles at a time. When you work on certain muscles, and they improve, it gives a sense of confidence and reward as well. This way, your brain starts believing in the process of working and getting results. That mentality promotes accelerated learning as well.

3. Endurance exercises

Endurance exercises are usually a combination of cardio, weightlifting and other forms of exercises. Such combinations let you work on your overall physical health. These exercises require greater mental involvement during the sessions.

The goal of endurance exercises is to keep pushing your limits every time you exercise. For instance, you can feel exhausted after working out for about 15 to 20 minutes constantly. But, regular exercise tends to increase endurance, and you can push your limits to 30, 40, 50 minutes and so on.

Depending on your physical state, you can choose a suitable combination of cardio, weightlifting and other forms of exercises.

4. Having some leisure time and resting

When you are disciplined about your other exercises, leisure and resting become a kind of exercise for your body. Meaning, the rest and leisure activities also help your body and brain improve regarding performance.

Leisure time means activities that you enjoy doing, such as going to events, meeting your friends, visiting a local park or any other. An activity you like is a great way to relax your mind and reenergize. However, remember that you need a disciplined rotation of exercising and leisure time during the week.

Along with leisure activities, taking breaks are as important as working out. Intense exercise without stopping can make you addicted to working out as well. Though not as dangerous as consuming alcohol, not resting can make you crave for more and more exercises. So, you can easily cross the limitation of healthy exercising.

Every time you indulge in an exercise session, it tears your muscle fibers, especially during weightlifting. Your immune system needs some time to work on the torn muscle fibers and repair them. If you do not give breaks to your muscles, the immune system keeps on working and repairing. It reaches a level when keeping up with the repair demand becomes impossible and that causes injuries. That is why experts suggest a cycle of exercising and taking breaks to promote a steady and useful growth of muscles.

Over-exercising leads to over physical and brain training, which is not good at all. You can feel restless and lose quality sleep. Your heart beats at an increased rate most of the time, which does not allow you to relax. This affects your ability to sleep at night. In addition, if you cannot sleep properly, your brain can't function properly during the day.

Therefore, breaks are as important as working out to maximize your physical and mental abilities safely.

Use physical fitness to increase your energy level, confidence and focus. Enjoy a healthy lifestyle to improve brain function for memory improvement. No need to dive into intense workout sessions. You should initiate your work light and gradually increase it towards intense levels. Moreover, keep yourself balanced regarding diet, workout, and breaks.

Chapter 8 – The Importance and Influence of Sleep

Just like your body needs rest from time to time, your brain requires rest too.

Why?

Your brain works every single second, no matter whether you are sleeping or awake. But the level of activity reduces to minimal when you are sleeping. Otherwise, you keep on thinking all the time, which requires your brain to work.

Every second, your brain remembers a million things such as memories, breathing, walking, talking, and so on. It all requires constant control of communication between brain cells. On an average, your brain can use 400 to 2000 calories on an average every day. This energy is utilized to manage body functions and memories.

Imagine yourself walking for a 100 miles without stopping. What if you do not allow your leg muscles to rest even after that? The same can be said for why the brain requires rest after conducting all the tasks every day.

Optimal rest is key to keeping your brain's performance. Without optimal sleep:

1. *Your memories start overlapping with each other*

There are three areas in your brain that work on memories -

hippocampus, prefrontal cortex and the parietal lobe.

These areas work on neural networks of memories when you sleep. So, sleeping strengthens your memories.

If you do not get optimal sleep, your brain does not get enough relaxed time to work on these neural networks. Most of the time, the brain has to focus on informational pieces you see around you. This starts overlapping one information with the other. You either forget things or remember it in a wrong way due to this.

2. *Your brain decreases in size*

Not enough research available, but experts believe that lack of sleep can reduce the size of the brain. Most affected areas include frontal, parietal and temporal lobes. They become smaller in size, which eventually impacts your brain function and other physical functions as you age.

3. *You lose control over emotions and feelings*

When you do not get enough sleep, your brain can't figure out what's going in the surroundings — the evaluation and analysis capacity decreases, which results in the misinterpretation of situations. So, even a minor issue becomes a mountain of problems, and you react irrationally.

You lose control over your anger and sadness. The brain lets you feel aggressive frequently, which can even lead to consequences you might regret after coming to your senses.

Sleep hygiene tips for quality sleep regularly

After knowing the importance of optimal sleep, you would want to ensure a good night's sleep. For that, you can focus on building a hygiene routine.

Sleep hygiene involves all kinds of behaviors you follow to get quality sleep every night.

1. Decide a fixed sleep routine

First and foremost, you need a fixed time when you go to bed and a fixed time when you leave your bed. This routine is a must if you want to subconsciously prepare your mind and body to sleep every night.

Initially, it would seem uncomfortable not being able to go to sleep right away. But you should keep going to bed at the same time every night. Eventually, your mind will start adjusting to the signs, and you will get the feeling of going to bed at the same time every night.

2. Avoid naps during the day

If you have naps for 15 to 20 minutes or longer during the day, it can affect your ability to sleep at night. Mostly, because your brain feels a false sense of relaxation. You can surely rest and relax, but avoid taking any naps during the day.

The naps also break the cycle of sleep routine you are trying to develop at night. Your brain does not know when to sleep if you keep having naps during the day. The initiation of quality sleep at night is easier if you avoid sleeping during the day.

3. Do not sit awake in bed

If you go to bed and stay awake for 10 to 20 minutes, it works against quality sleep. But this is pretty common among people. Mostly, we all tend to fall into the cycle of thoughts that happen during that day. Or, our concerns, worries, insecurities and other emotions get a chance to appear on the surface of consciousness.

In such conditions, you should not stay in bed. Otherwise, your brain will start associating the bed with worries, thought processing and information analysis. You do not want that! So, get out and take a walk in your living area, sit on a couch or a chair as long as you do not feel the need to sleep. Make sure you do not give yourself any sort of entertainment through television, mobile phone, or other gadgets. Be with your thoughts as long as they do not indulge you to choose a negative path.

4. Do not use your bed to watch television, reading or work

If you use your bed for activities such as watching TV, reading or working at night, it loses the impact on your brain. So, even when you do want to sleep and go to bed, your brain does not feel cozy enough.

Associate your bed with sleeping only to set the mood right.

5. Avoid substances that counter sleep

Sleep fragmentation does not let you get enough rest period. Your brain does not reach the state of deep sleep due to substances such as alcohol, cigarettes and certain medications. So, you need to stay as far away from them as possible.

6. Develop an exercise routine

You have already understood the importance of exercising in a balanced manner. Regular exercise also improves your ability to have quality sleep. The increased quantity of endorphins in your body helps in the initiation of sleep when you go to bed.

7. Create a comfortable and quiet bedroom

The atmosphere and feeling of your bedroom matter a lot to get quality sleep. Generally, there are two major aspects you need to consider- comfort and quietness.

To create a comfortable environment, you can work on the temperature first. Make sure the room's thermostat creates a convenient temperature in the room. Try aiming for a cooler atmosphere instead of making it warmer.

Along with the temperature, you can switch off all the bright lights and make it darker. Bright lights are not helpful in the bedroom at night. If you do not feel comfortable about complete darkness, you can keep a dim bulb on for the night. Also, choose a comfortable mattress to give your body proper comfort to promote sleep.

To ensure quietness, you need to switch off the television, if you have one in the bedroom. Also, put your phone in silent mode, so the unwanted notifications do not bother you at night. At the same time, try making your bedroom doors and windows partially soundproof. If there are pets that make noises, keep them out of your bedroom at night.

8. Practice yoga and deep breathing before going to bed

One good habit you can develop is meditating before going to bed at night. Just for 10 to 15 minutes, you can relax and remove all thoughts from your mind and focus on deep breathing. Inhale through your nose and exhale through your mouth. This will relax your mind and prepare for a wonderful sleep every night.

9. Have a warm shower

If it suits you, a warm shower before bed also relaxes and promotes sleep. You can make it a habit and push yourself initially to the shower. After a few days, your body will ask for a shower every night before bed.

10. Have caffeine with caution

In this same book, you have read how caffeine alerts your brain and increases your mental attention. However, these things are not effective when you are trying to sleep at night.

The fact that caffeine stays in your system for a few hours makes it important to drink it with caution. If you drink too much coffee or sugary soda drinks a few hours before going to bed, it interrupts in sleep initiation.

In the short-term, caffeine works as a stimulator for your central nervous system. You feel alert within 10 to 20 minutes of having caffeine, depending on the quantity. Its effect stays for about 6 or more hours.

Suppose, you drink a cup of coffee, containing 200 mg of caffeine at 6 p.m. Then, at 11 p.m., your body will still have about 100 mg of caffeine in the system. This is a big reason why coffee drinkers fail to get quality sleep at night.

Moderate caffeine amount during the early hours of the day is beneficial. Your mind can encode short-term memories more efficiently due to the increased alertness boosted due to adrenaline — the heart rate increases, which sends more oxygen to your brain allowing enhanced productivity. But in the long-term, high caffeine consumption leads to lack of sleep or lack of quality sleep. You lose the ability to go to deep sleep at night, which does not allow your mind to relax effectively.

The best thing you can do is choose the right quantity and time to have coffee and other beverages that contain caffeine. Always restrict your coffee consumption after 2 p.m. This way, the caffeine will fade away in your system by the time you reach your bed. Also, keep the amount moderate up to 1 to 2 cups only.

Myths about Sleep and Memory

Now, let's debunk some common myths people have about sleep and memory.

Myth #1 - Memories do not go anywhere just because you do not sleep.

This is probably the biggest myth out there among common people. Most people do not find any logic between memories and sleeping. How can staying awake make your long-term memories go away? But that happens. Consistent cases of insomnia can lead to the shrinkage of the hippocampus and other areas of your brain.

Your brain loses the ability to study the surroundings properly, which influences memory encoding. The wrong information encoding in the first place does not allow your brain to think rationally or make correct neural networks. So, you either cannot memorize or memorize things incorrectly.

Plus, the level of toxins such as cortisol increases, which leads to other health issues too. So, not sleeping can impact your ability to make short-term and long-term memories.

Myth #2 - My optimal sleep period is 6 hours only.

Generally, optimal sleep period is 7 to 8 hours for most people. Only a few people have different biological conditions that allow them to get all the health benefits with less sleep.

However, most people these days sleep less and think that they are sleeping enough. This happens due to the conditioning of our brain with time. People tend to sleep for about 6 hours or less and feel normal because of the adaptation of their mental state. But it still damages your brain all the time.

Just because you wake up using an alarm and drink a coffee, it does not compensate for the lack of sleep you get. Such people perform their everyday tasks in a reduced mental state, which keeps on declining the mental performance.

Myth #3 - I can complete my sleep at the end of the week.

Many people go to bed late and wake up early during 4 to 5 days of the week. Moreover, they think that the lack of sleep is coverable during the weekends. But sleeping does not work that way! Our body and mind requires a consistent routine of sleeping and staying awake to feel fresh. Otherwise, we tend to feel tired all the time.

Plus, people, who change their sleeping patterns during weekdays and weekends, experience a kind of jet-lag experience. Their body and brain become confused about the time zones, which increases memory issues, irrational thinking, and tiredness.

Sleeping a little longer during weekends is fine, but you can't expect it to cover the deprivation caused due to the long-term habit of early mornings and late nights.

Myth #4 - I can always have a sleeping pill to get good quality sleep.

Not at all. People think why to bother with sleep hygiene when you can have one pill and sleep for the whole night.

That does not happen. Sure, people look asleep after taking a sleeping pill. But that sleep is not natural. Using a sleeping pill does not allow your brainwaves to reach the level of deep sleep. You simply stay sedated for the whole night without getting the real benefits of deep sleep.

That is why sleep induction with medication is not a healthy solution. Some studies suggest that sleeping pills negatively impact the connections between brain cells. Hence, you gradually lose learning ability and memory holding capacity.

Chapter 9 – Studying Hard Is Old School, Study Smart for Exams

If you are a dedicated student, 24 hours in a day do not seem enough to manage everything. You have assignments, projects, and classes to cover. Between all that, you have to find time to effectively prepare for exams. Then, there is your social life, commitments, and other activities.

Studying hard for exams has always been a common concept. However, you can study SMART by understanding your brain and utilizing that knowledge in your study patterns.

This chapter will tell you how concentration and focus are achievable conveniently if you target studying strategically. A strategy that does not just appeal to your syllabus, but also to your brain's ability to perform.

1. Find different ways to learn one topic

Your brain has different kinds of sensitivities. Different forms of information source stimulate different sections of your brain. So, it seems logical that you can understand a topic more effectively if you consume it through different modes.

Modern-education system allows you to obtain the same study material in the text, audio, video, and other forms. So, you can study one topic in different modes to create a strong map of information in your mind. Furthermore, you can increase knowledge retention by talking about a topic. Helping your friend understand a topic can also help you strengthen that information in your brain.

One important thing to remember is the distribution of different learning modes. Do not sit down to complete all the workload in one go. Divide the process for a distributed time period and consume one-by-one for better results.

2. Pick multiple different subjects every day

If you take one subject and take a deep dive in a single day, that is not a smart move. Similar information going in your brain can easily overlap with each other and make incorrect memories.

To save yourself from misinterpretation, you need to choose multiple different subjects to study on a daily basis. You can pick suitable sections, which you can cover easily and do them one-by-one.

Also, try to pick very different topics together such as physics, history, and literature. This way, you will be able to avoid information overlap in your brain.

3. Follow a periodic schedule of reviewing

You have seen in this book how reviewing is a great tool to help your brain strengthen a memory. You can apply that to your exam preparations as well. Periodic and distributed revision is effective to retain the learned topics.

You need to develop a distributed reviewing schedule for every topic you study. This way, you can transfer it to the level of long-term memory.

Commonly, you can select 5 reviews after studying a topic. Divide those reviews into intervals such as 1 day, 3 days, 7 days, 30 days, and 45 days.

4. Minimize distractions

If your mind is focused (or not so focused) on two or more things at once, the productivity reduces. There is no such thing as multitasking. In theory, multitasking means focusing your brain in doing two things. This is not impossible but it does not help when you need to concentrate on one thing. For instance, you can walk, read and listen to music at once, but that just distracts you from grasping the details of content you're reading.

Solving mathematical problems while watching TV, answering messages on your phone and checking your social media profiles. This is not the way to study smarter.

You need to create a comfortable environment for studying by minimizing the distractions. So, your phone needs to go on silent mode, if not switching it off. You can at least turn off the access to the internet for the time being.

When working on a computer, keep the tabs minimal. Keep books and notes that you need in front of you at that moment. The less clutter, the better.

5. Connect new information with existing memories and learnings

This is the biggest approach to improve your ability to learn and retain knowledge. New concepts are easier to learn when you connect them to existing memory.

For instance, your existing knowledge of water current can help you understand the concepts of electricity. Battery works as a water pump, water current is the electric current, and voltage can replace the water pressure.

Similarly, you can understand the antibodies of the human body with the concept of war. Just like soldiers, antibodies in our body fight alien particles to keep the body protected from diseases.

This is a great way of learning concretely and developing memory connections that last for a long time.

6. Use your eyes and voice when reading

When you read, seeing the text just stimulates one memory sensitivity of your brain. You can double the impact by including your auditory sensibility.

Read notes aloud once and keep highlighting important statements.

Then, you can go through the highlighted portions once again, reading them out loud. This will allow your brain to grasp the important information properly.

7. Take a break once in a while

You need breaks from your study. No matter how vast your syllabus seems, you can fit in regular breaks with a well-established system. Breaks will allow your brain to relax, which improves focus and enhances clarity of thoughts.

Instead of studying for hours, give yourself small breaks of 5-10 minutes, after every 45 to 60 minutes of studying. This sense of break can also become a distraction if you keep looking at the clock to reach your 10-minute break. So, use a stopwatch for this purpose.

Another important thing is how you utilize your break. Picking up your smartphone or using a computer will not help you relax at all. The purpose is giving your mind some time to relax. So, you need to stay away from any devices. You can sit with your thoughts or walk.

8. Set positive rewards for a good study session

Before you begin your daily study session, decide a reward in your mind. A positive reward such as eating healthy food you like, playing your favorite musical instrument, going out for skateboarding or anything else.

This will become a positive reinforcement for your brain to concentrate. The sense of reward is a big deal for your brain and it enhances productivity.

After completing a study session, you can enjoy that pre-decided reward. This will relax your mind and motivate for the next day as well.

9. Believe the process

Let us get it out there - the difference between average students and successful students.

An average student decides his or her performance goals. But students that find success in their education usually tend to focus on learning goals.

This small diversion from performance to learning makes a big difference.

You concentrate more on learning important concepts rather than thinking about obtaining 98% on your upcoming math test.

You give yourself daily learning tasks and master problem-solving ability. So, high scores come along automatically.

It is true that most education centers give importance to exam scores. Nevertheless, as a student, you need to define your learning path. If successful, you will not have to worry about exam scores.

When preparing for exams, have faith in a disciplined process of learning. Follow your approach and work on weak and strong subjects from time to time. Embrace more challenges and push yourself to improve.

10. Designate a fixed learning space

You have to have a fixed study area at home — a place where you only go to study your subjects. Studying anywhere or everywhere works fine, but it does not allow your brain to feel organized.

On the other hand, having a single place for studying allows your brain to get in the learning zone immediately. One organized study area also automatically becomes a memory palace in your mind. Your brain creates a mind map of that study area and keeps all the valuable studied material there. This way, you can memorize faster and keep those memories in the long-term memory zone.

Chapter 10 – Bring Your A-game at Work

If you are a professional, your office is the one place where you are supposed to be sharp, concentrated and productive.

But the workplace is also a place packed with distracting activities. So, it creates a contradicting scenario for people who want to bring their A-game and perform.

Staying focused and sharp at work is about working on your memory and brain function. You want to reduce the stress levels so that your work does not become a pile of mess for you.

At the same time, you want to improve your memory and remember important information, names, dates, passwords and other things. This will surely reduce stress and save time when working. Feeling positive and thinking faster can also make a huge difference in your workplace productivity.

All these enhancements can improve self-confidence. In addition, guess what! It is all possible with some easy changes.

How to keep your mind sharp at work?

1. Switch tasks

You already know how memories are divided into short-term and long-term. So, use that knowledge and trigger both kinds of memories when working.

You usually focus on your long-term memories by following the same procedures at work. How about switching tasks to activate short-term memories more often. You can pair a task that you do daily with a task you have not done ever.

This will give a sort of challenge to your brain and activate most neural networks. You will be learning and using your existing skills at the same time.

A flexible approach to work keeps our mood fresh. Our brain can focus on different things one after another and concentrate better. So, you can feel on top of your game all day long.

2. Find new social groups to hang out with

Do you go out with your office friends only? If all your buddies belong to the same profession, you are limiting your social mingling opportunities. People who share the same profession tend to have a similar broad point of view. Your mind needs to feel challenged to evolve and get sharper.

For that, you need to find new social groups to hang out with. Make friends who do not have the same profession as yours. Interacting with new people will give you new perspectives. Your mind will have to find different assumptions, blind spots of thoughts and biases.

This way, you can enhance your viewpoint and discover new ways to see opportunities and solutions for the same problems. Not just at work, but also in life!

3. Find your best work hours

We all are different concerning productivity and concentration. Some people feel at their best in the morning, while others need a few hours of steady pace to pick up. You need to find out what sort of performance you have regarding productivity.

Then, you can choose your peak productivity hours for important tasks of the day. This will give you a chance to utilize the best work hours without stressing too much. You can schedule important meetings and discussions during peak performance hours for maximum results.

4. Take a break

Just like students, professionals also need breaks after consistent working periods. This can depend on your mindset, stress levels and work in hand. No need to make a set routine, but it is important to make sure that you do not overwork. Whenever possible, give yourself 15-20 minutes of free time. You can relax with a cup of coffee, talk to your colleagues, or go out of the office for a walk.

Even if work is too much and you cannot go out for 20 minutes, simply stand up and stretch your body. This would not take more than 1 to 2 minutes. You will surely feel refreshed and ready to finish that work in hand.

5. Pick one task at a time

Instead of multitasking, you should approach work with monotasking. No matter how packed your day seems, quality, productive results are possible only with monotasking. You can make things more organized by making a list of tasks and creating a mental strategy of how you can do it all.

6. Eat tangy fruits

Tangy fruits such as oranges contain vitamin C, which has plenty of health benefits. But the citrus taste of such fruits also allows your brain to feel alert immediately. You can have a glass of orange juice if you are particularly feeling out of focus at work.

7. Watch a funny video

Of course, you do not want to waste your precious time at work. But a single video of a funny cat or dog can cheer you up. Then, you can double your focus level and work more productively.

Sometimes, constant work leads to boredom. You start resenting a work which you love doing. That is why you need a mood booster to energize your brain for another session of productive work. Watching a funny video for even 5 to 10 minutes can give that boost and help you up your game again.

8. Utilize 20-20-20 method

This method is a quick solution to reduce overstimulation and overstressed scenarios at work. Most people can't take long breaks when the workload is too much. In such situations, you can utilize this method to reduce stress levels.

The method involves staring at an object, which is 20 feet away from your desk. Stare at the object for 20 seconds. You have to do this after every 20 minutes of consistent work. Hence, it is called 20-20-20 method.

This is a great exercise to keep your eyes and brain away from the computer for a while.

9. Schedule meetings after 1 pm

If a meeting is important, you have to prepare in advance for that. Early-morning appointments and meetings seem to begin a day with high-stress levels. You feel hurried during the morning period, which makes you feel stressed during that whole day.

To save yourself from the morning stress, always try to set your important meetings after 1 pm. This will give you enough time to prepare and keep your mind calm.

10. Consider deep breathing

Deep breathing works on your mind and body together. You can use this exercise to whenever you feel stress on your mind and increased heart rate. Give good 5 minutes of inhaling and exhaling air.

Inhale through your nose and exhale through your mouth. Do it slowly and repeat by focusing only on your breathing. After a few breaths, your mind will start getting the rhythm and focusing on the air going in and coming out. The heart rate will calm down, and your mind will feel relaxed.

And when you feel relaxed, you can get more work done productively.

11. Stop notifications

One sound of "bling" on your phone can bring you back from a focused mindset. Looking at notifications on your phone can't keep you productive. But you can't put your phone on silent mode like a student. Important people call you during the office hours.

So, you need to smartly minimize the distracting notifications. For instance, log out from all the social media profiles or put their notifications on silent to avoid unnecessary alerts. This way, you can avoid the temptation of looking at your phone constantly after every few minutes. You stay aware of the work in hand, which enhances your productivity.

12. Spend 10 minutes every morning strategizing

A rough strategy in your mind can give you a plan for the day. Our brain likes to work strategically. People, who sit and start typing buttons on their computer right away, tend to work less productively. Smart people sit and give 10 minutes to overviewing every task first, then, choose a sequence of doing those tasks.

You can do this and become more efficient at work without putting too much pressure. At the end of one task, your mind can smoothly switch to another. Hence, you can make your office hours smooth and productive, without putting too much pressure on your mind.

13. Go home with no work

These days, people have forgotten the difference between home and office. Laptops and smartphones allow you to work 24 hours. But you have to pay the price regarding your mental productivity. Your mind has its limits, so you can't work beyond 8 hours. Plus, your home should be a place where you feel relaxed. If the stress of work comes to your home as well, your mind won't feel calm anywhere.

That is why you need to leave your work at an office, whenever you stand up to go back home. Sure, some exceptions are possible. But you should try never to bring work back home.

14. Practice eating with chopsticks

Eating with chopsticks is not an easy task, especially for beginners. It takes your mental alertness and complete focus initially to pick food with two chopsticks and eat. You can dedicate one meal to this method of eating. This will become a fun exercise for your brain to learn alertness and improve concentration.

If you already feel comfortable about chopsticks, use your non-dominant hand for the same activity. The left side of the brain controls the right side of the body and vice versa. Using your non-dominant hand will further activate your brain function.

15. Use new routes to your workplace

When you follow the same route and commute for years, it puts your brain on an autopilot mode. The brain does not have to do much to take you to your workplace and bring back.

How about you give a little stimulation to your brain first thing in the morning! Leave home early enough and pick a new, unfamiliar route to your office. This will activate hippocampus and cortex areas because your brain will start encoding the new visible information.

Along with the route, you can also change the mode of commute. Try switching from cars to bike and even walking if possible. Designate a day of the week when you take public transportation to reach office and come back.

These new changes to your routes and commute will make you feel more focused and alert.

16. Learn and practice cooking

People do not look at it that way, but cooking is a great exercise for your brain.

When cooking, all your senses become alert. You see and touch ingredients, hear the sound of cooking food, smell its aroma and taste from time to time. Moreover, every ingredient has to go in the right amount. So, your brain keeps on analyzing and evaluating the quantities. All this makes cooking a comprehensive mental exercise. In addition, the amazing part is that most people feel good about cooking once or twice a week.

You can choose cooking as a weekend hobby and indulge in making new dishes to stimulate all memory sensitivities of your brain.

17. Pick low-tech days

If you can face a tsunami, a swimming pool can never make you afraid. Meaning, you can upgrade your mental capacity picking hard things and doing them successfully.

We all rely on technology in one way or the other to manage our life and work. So that becomes the best thing to challenge yourself. You can choose one suitable day during weekends as your low-tech day. If you need to reach out to your friends, you can go directly to them, or memorize their phone numbers and call via public telephone booths.

Similarly, you can find your ways without using a GPS. Grab a map or ask locals to reach an address. See how many tasks you can do with minimal use of technology. This will make you confident and improve your mind's capacity to resolve problems faster.

Other important habits you already know about:

- You need to get enough sleep to keep your brain at its maximum capacity.

- Keep yourself physically active throughout the day to ensure mental activity.

- Avoid bad habits such as smoking and limit your consumption of alcohol and caffeine.

- Develop the best-suited diet for your body and mind.

As a student, you keep learning new things, but this newness in learning reduces as you move to professional life. Sometimes, you need to make proactive efforts to challenge yourself. You need to find new things that can help you activate your short-term memory senses. Volunteering, working on a new skill and choosing new projects to work on. New learning is always a reliable method of keeping your brain sharp.

Along with that, you should try and involve most of your senses when working. The more senses involved, the better your brain can create long-lasting memories with them. Do not just see things, allow your brain to use the sense of smell, touch, taste and hear whenever possible. Of course, this is not possible when you are working in front of a computer. That is why a hobby matters, with which you can utilize all your senses. Playing golf, going to dance classes, and other hobbies can help activate your brain's maximum performance.

Many people start forgetting things because they believe in forgetting. If you have faith that you will forget things because you are aging, it will happen. You have to have a different kind of faith that you can keep your brain function in top-notch condition. Your memory preservation capacity stays secure if you keep learning and follow a healthy lifestyle. Along with that, a positive mindset is also important to keep your cognitive functions to its optimal state.

To improve your memory holding capacity, you can apply repeating tasks. A task or information, which is completely new, requires repetition. Say information out loud three times to memorize and do a task 3 times during different times of a day. Repeat to create a strong memory of doing something, until your brain attains an autopilot mode.

When repeating something, try to distribute it in a long period. Repeating in a short period will not do any good if you want to memorize a method of using new software - space out the practice time. Practice once, then, repeat every day once only to get in the zone of basic usability. After attaining enough confidence, you will become ready to use that software for your daily tasks.

Chapter 11 – Mistakes and Learning: How to Get Fastest Results

There are two ways to learn something:

Either you make no mistake and aim for perfectionism.

Or, you make mistakes and learn in the process.

So, which one would be the best pathway to learning most efficiently?

Believe or not, perfectionism can become a self-defeating approach in a learning process.

Look at it this way - the existence of life is about surviving by adapting and being flexible with the external scenarios. That is how human species have survived and evolved. But what does perfectionism do? It contradicts with the concept of survival by making rigidifying expectations.

Perfectionism is usually a result of social surroundings and expectations of others. What begins as tiny expectations for parents, tend to destroy abilities if your brain gets hardwired to aim for perfection.

To understand this better, you should know what perfectionism is.

Perfectionism is a type of personality that seeks the highest performance standards and absolute flawlessness. Anything less than perfect is not acceptable by such personalities. Such people tend to become more critical about their performance and other people's performance as well. They constantly stay in an evaluation mode. It all seems fine until it doesn't!

Perfectionism has its serious side effects that can stop you from learning new things in the first place.

1. Even tiny mistakes cause unbearable stress

A perfectionist personality cannot handle mistakes. Even small mistakes impact them hard and put them in a stressed mode. The brain easily loses the broad picture and starts focusing on that one mistake only. Mostly, such people divert from their goals and stay focused on resolving unnecessary mistakes. This increases the time of learning things.

2. Wasting time becomes unavoidable

A perfectionist person is unlikely to move ahead without resolving all the problems present currently. This is harmful when you have a set deadline to learn something or complete a project. Absolute perfection is almost impossible in most things we do in our lives. So, such people waste a lot of time without considering the importance of time efficiency.

3. Procrastination comes along

You might not suspect a perfectionist to delay his processes, but it happens very often mostly because a perfectionist looks for the best resources, time, place and conditions to start something. This regressively opens the gates of procrastination and do not allow the initiation of a learning process.

4. Slow development of self-loathing

It is common for perfectionists to not feel good enough and self-criticize. The person finds imperfections in his or her work. Those imperfections keep on coming repeatedly, which instills a belief of limited abilities. The person starts thinking that he or she can't ever achieve the perfect results. This belief in failure sets the path to not being able to learn anything.

Perfectionism and Psychological Distress

If perfectionism becomes a part of the psyche, you tend to develop a pervasive approach to learning. Trying new things becomes a daunting task because you assume that you are going to fail. Your unachievable expectations do not allow you to take new challenges. So, your hidden abilities stay hidden.

Self-focused understanding is another issue with perfectionism. You think about your performance all the time. Which is why new learning opportunities come and go without gaining any of your attention. With that, you keep on losing your ability to innovate, create new things and adapt to the growing world around you.

Moreover, perfectionism can become a continuous source of unwanted emotions. Staring at your report card for hours or thinking about one remark made by a senior at work all day long. All these things make you feel anxious, depressed and frustrated. And none of it is helpful in learning new things.

Every mistake becomes equivalent to failing. You believe that you are losing respect due to your mistakes, even when the errors are not so big in the first place. Personal standards become so high that you lose the hope of ever achieving them. You doubt every decision, every step you take towards your goal. And that does not let you stay productive or efficient.

Setting high standards is not perfectionism. Most successful people start by setting a high standard where they want to reach. Self-destructive nature of perfectionism lies in the concern you feel about your mistakes. High standards are supposed to keep you motivated and take you to the desired success. But some people feel so worried about mistakes that they tend to punish themselves with concerns and doubts. Because a perfectionist becomes a self-critic, he or she assumes that other people are also thinking the same. This gradually makes that person reluctant towards new activities, projects, and opportunities.

Perfectionism gives a bad feeling about mistakes, which interrupts the gradual process of learning. All sorts of learnings in life involves mistakes. Seeking excellence is about enjoying the mistakes along with the learning process until you reach the desired goals. But perfectionism does not let you have that enjoyment. You forget about a 100 things you are doing right and find one or more mistakes somehow to loathe yourself.

For example, if a perfectionist student moves from a grade C to grade B, he will not feel good about it because he wanted Grade A in the first place. For him, the goal is to get grade A, no matter if he can retain the learned knowledge or not. That is the problem with perfectionism! They forget about the real value of learning new things.

This is why perfectionists conceal most of their mistakes from people, who can give genuine feedback. They do not let their mistakes come out, which does not allow them to gain crucial insights. If a student of literature avoids showing written work to teachers, he or she can't improve. Hence, the performance in exams keeps on going down. The same goes for people working in an office and hiding mistakes from their seniors.

How to Use Mistakes When Learning

Instead of being a perfectionist, you should think about being a high achiever. Do not be afraid of the mistakes, use them!

Just like a small mistake haunts a perfectionist, the same mistake becomes a learning tool for a high achiever.

To acquire that approach, you need to pass the feeling of panic, inconvenience, and embarrassment. Everyone is making mistakes, and everyone is fine. Do not stress over a mistake because it happened. Learn why it happened, and do not let it happen again. That is how you can utilize mistakes in your learning process.

A mistake is not equivalent to failing. You fail when you waste your time in the wrong ways of doing things. A mistake is just a single wrong action. So, you can shift your path to the right ways and obtain success in learning.

How to do it?

1. Take the ownership of your mistakes

First, you need to own the mistakes you have made. Owning is about accepting the mistake to yourself first. Then, you need to make sure that everyone who needs to know about it knows. Be proactive and tell every relevant person about the mistakes you have made. Do not put excuses in it, simply acknowledge the mistake and apologize. Also, convey that you are working to resolve the problem.

If a mistake does not concern anyone except you, no need to tell anybody, in fact, you should not even think about what other people "may be" thinking.

In your mind, or to others, never try to blame your mistake on others. Accepting your mistakes is a sign of integrity and courage. Even if other people around you do not think so, you should have faith in the power of accepting mistakes. When you attain your goal and resolve the mistake, people will remember you for your integrity and courage.

If you keep ignoring your mistakes, you can't work on them ever. So, accept your mistakes if you want to learn something, anything!

2. *Learn to reframe your mistakes*

It is common for all of us to feel a little shocked or embarrassed about a mistake at first. But this negative light should shine for an initial period only. Otherwise, you will start self-loathing like a perfectionist.

What you need to learn is an ability to reframe the way you look at your mistakes. Instead of evaluating yourself, start evaluating the reasons why that mistake occurred. Try to remove the emotional aspect from this evaluation. Treat your mistake as a conclusion of certain actions. Your job is to analyze those actions to discover the real problem.

This approach will increase your knowledge and bring you closer to your learning goals. At the same time, you will feel motivated to resolve the problems and move forward.

For example, suppose you were working on a project, and the results are full of mistakes. In that case, you can go through the process you used and find the loopholes. Maybe you did not invest time in the ongoing testing of the project. So, the solution would be the introduction of a planned testing method. You can also include a checklist of every step to monitor the progress of your project.

The idea is to lean towards your productive side no matter what mistakes you make in the process. Every situation, positive or negative, can benefit you one or the other if you have the right approach. Unfortunately, the opposite version is also true. You can destroy a good or bad situation without your negative approach.

It is all about your mindset towards mistakes. They happen, and they will happen! All you can do is keep a productive mindset. So, whenever a mistake appears, you can productively go through it without stopping at all.

But remember, you can't be too OK about making mistakes. You are supposed to have a positive approach, not a careless approach. Take the mistakes responsibly and learn from it.

3. Analyze mistakes objectively

In the previous point, you got a glimpse of how to look at the objective side of mistakes. Here is how you can do it:

- Think about the objectives you wanted to achieve.
- Note the wrong actions you made in the process.
- Find out the time when it all went wrong.
- Make a list of reasons why you made mistakes.

Again, it is important to stay on the objective side of this analysis. Asking yourself "why" can easily take you to the emotional lane of making mistakes. Do not let it happen. Be honest and choose the objective side of every reason behind the mistakes.

4. Put your conclusions into practice

If you analyze and do nothing, it will not help. There is always a feeling that pulls us back to the regular, habitual tasks. Resist that and work on the conclusions you attain after analyzing your mistakes. This is a key step to learn something and memory improvement. If you quit, you break the process of growing your mental capacity and skills.

Most of the time, the necessary steps involve changes in your habits or surroundings. You need motivation and self-discipline to make those changes, or it all goes to the self-sabotaging mode. The benefits of mistakes require these changes if you do not want to get stuck with limited knowledge or skills.

Moving forward, you need to find out the resources, knowledge, skills or tools required to avoid those mistakes this time. Do not seek quick fixes as they do not last. Think about finding a permanent solution so that you never make that mistake again. If you have to commit to a new habit forever, do it in the name of disciplined learning.

When learning, most mistakes are personal ones. This enhances the importance of giving a deadline to yourself to implement the required changes. You can't take forever in fixing one mistake. Decide a fixed timescale and be disciplined enough to follow that timescale.

The type of tools will depend on the mistakes and their causes. For example, if your mistakes were a result of forgetfulness, you need to work on your memory by using accelerated learning tools and techniques. Giving importance to details need to become a part of your habit. Plus, you need to become more organized to remember things. For that, you will require handy pre-planned strategies to work with.

Similarly, if you are constantly failing to deliver quality work to your clients, you and your team have to work on improving communication channels. Some mistakes are organizational rather than personal. But they can equally impact your ability to learn new skills. You have to become more creative about such mistakes. Try including other people associated with that mistake and find creative personal ways of conquering it at the same time.

Making a small or big change is a required action to resolve mistakes. These changes are important, so you have to be willing to adapt. Also, do not feel scared to ask for help. If you have people who can help in the process, always approach them. Most people feel good about helping others. But you have to be ready to take the ultimate steps. Others can only provide tools or encourage you; the ultimate change has to come from you.

5. Monitor your progress

It is "monitor" your progress, not "feel worried" about it. A successful upgrade after a mistake allows you to prevent the old mistakes at least. The goal is surely to make minimal mistakes, which is why you should monitor your progress regularly. Find out if the implemented actions are working in your favor or not. Evaluate to ensure that you aren't making the same kinds of mistakes. If possible, you can also choose a reliable person to keep an eye on your actions and mistakes. This will help in staying committed to the task of learning.

Key takeaways

Making mistakes is a common habit. Punishing yourself for mistakes is not a solution. Perfectionism can lead to the wrong way of learning. It does not allow you to learn, as you keep thinking about the negative emotions cultivated due to impossible expectations.

Owning your mistakes and working on them objectively is the fastest way to learn anything. You save yourself from the negative emotions and stress and allow your brain to learn skills, resources, knowledge, and tools.

So, aim not to repeat the same mistakes. Try and become a higher achiever instead of being a perfectionist.

Chapter 12 – What You May Not Be Aware Of

Have you ever marched into a room full of confidence and all of a sudden forgot why you came in there in the first place? If so, you will understand that the human memory is full of marvel. We often forget the very important information and yet we remember millions of useless details we will never even need. Why is it so? Here are 7 of the most surprising and strangest facts about human memory. Let's have a look at all these in detail:

1. *There is essentially no limit to the amount of info that you can remember.*

Considering how much we tend to forget on a daily basis, it may come out as strange. However, it is true that our mind has a virtually unlimited 'storage capacity' to learn. A rough calculation done by Paul Reber, the Professor of Psychology at Northwest University indicates that the brain can store about 2.5 petabytes of data, which is 2,500,000 GB or say, 300 years' worth of television.

"The brain consists of around 1 billion neurons. Every neuron makes about thousand links to the other neurons, which amounts to above a trillion links. The neurons come together so that each one of them can aid in some memories at one time, exponentially enhancing the memory storage capacity of the brain to something closer to about 2.5 Petabytes."

Hence, if we have an essentially unlimited storage capacity, why do we still obliterate so much? This is a huge topic, which is worthy of its post. However, a lot of pieces of evidence suggest that we are more likely to commemorate something if we make an active and bustling effort of understanding it and if we come across it on a regular basis - as this strengthens the links between the neurons in the brain & makes information simpler to recall.

2. Nonetheless, we can only learn and memorize only a handful of things in our 'short-term' memory

A huge part of the reason that we seem to forget a lot of things may well be that, even though our long-term memory is essentially limitless, our short-term 'working' memory has a very small capacity. The initial research into the short-term memory suggests that we can only remember five to nine pieces of information there at a given time. Nonetheless, some more recent experiments have suggested that it may even be as low as just four!

Still not convinced?

You can try it out yourself with a quick experiment. Given below is a list of words, which you need to study for two minutes. Then, write down as many words as you remember from the list, without looking.

- Nine
- Plugs
- Army
- Clock
- Desk

- Swap
- Lamp
- Bank
- Horse
- Hold
- Cell
- Apple
- Fire
- Color
- Find
- Ring
- Table
- Hold
- Baby
- Bird
- Lust
- Sway
- Worm
- Sword
- Rock

This confinement on the short-term memory explains why 'sloshing' the information just before an examination does not work very well. Hence, one clear strategy of remembering more of what you learn is to "space out" your studying. By this, more information is moved from your 'short-term' to your 'long-term' memory.

3. *Studying or acquiring new information makes physical modifications in the structure of your brain.*

It is quite easy to think of the brain as a magical box in which your memories, emotions, and thoughts are stored. However, when it comes down to it, the brain is just a part of your body like your muscles and your heart. Exercising your brain in particular ways, whether it is learning some new skills like a musical instrument or some new language, or simply just learning the things from any book produces the physical changes in the structure of the brain.

Thanks to the contemporary imaging techniques like MRI, i.e. Magnetic Resonance Imaging, scientists are able to see these modifications before and after the learning takes place. Additionally, they have found not just the major enhancements in the activity (which is measured by the blood flow) in the particular areas of the brain linked with the activities, but also the long-lasting structural modifications concerning grey and white matter.

4. *Being able to approach the information quickly on the internet makes you less in favor of remembering it.*

It is always better to access any information in just a few seconds and the resources like Google, YouTube and Wikipedia have been the major parts of an insurgency in how we find the information. However, studies have suggested that there is an interesting adverse effect of being able to access the information in such a convenient way. If your brain is aware that it can simply re-access it in this easy manner, it is less likely even to bother to remember the info itself!

We do not try to store the information in our memory to the same level that we have always used to. It is because now we know that internet knows almost everything. Anyone can contemplate that this limits the personal memories. Constantly looking at this vast world through the lens of our smartphone cameras can result in us believing our smartphones to store our memories for us. In this way, we are paying less attention to the life itself and are becoming even worse at remembering the events from our own lives.

This phenomenon is now called 'The Google Effect' and has become part of a continuous debate as to whether the internet is making us dull and dumb.

5. *We are capable of remembering things, which did not even take place.*

As time passes, it can become difficult to know how precise our memories of any event are. Certainly, for a lot of our childhood memories, it can be a little hard to know for sure whether we are remembering the director, the primary event itself, or are just recalling some story which our parents told us or from the home videos or from photos from that time.

However, this concept has a much scarier connection, which has been studied by psychologists. In one experiment, interviewers were able to persuade seventy percent of the people that they had committed a crime when in actuality they had not.

This has very big implications for the legal system, and on the way the eyewitness testimony is used in the court. It provides other amazing insights into how the human brains work.

6. Testing oneself on the information is better than just re-reading or rehearsing it.

The term 'test' is as the case may be, up there with the 'public speaking,' regarding its ability to certainly terrify the people. Nobody likes tests, and even the educational professionals argue that people are 'tested' away too much and apparently, it is getting in the way of the 'real' education. Of course, there is an often cited quote in the education circles, which goes something like this-

"You do not fatten a pig by continually weighing it."

Along with the amount of compulsory national tests, which the students are expected to take in today's time, it is hard to argue with. Nonetheless, research shows that consistent 'low-stakes' tests can be immensely advantageous in the whole learning process. Instead of constantly being pampered and catered the information by re-reading it in the same book, testing charges us confront the gaps in the knowledge, and makes our brains work harder for retrieving any information. In doing so, it also strengthens the neuronal links & makes it simpler to retrieve in the future. The brain, in this way, is just like any muscles in the body: you have to exercise for it to remain stronger.

There are some reasons to begin testing yourself on what all you have learned right away!

7. (Nearly) Forgetting Something Makes It More Likely To Be Remembered.

Partially forgetting something & then striving to remember it is an essential part of the process of memory formation. When we struggle to remember things, we are exercising our brain & telling it that 'This information is critical, store it somewhere very safe and easily available.' This is the main concept behind the 'spaced repetition' approach.

The information is re-visited in set intervals for strengthening the memory of it in this study technique. The concept is that you re-visit any information when you have almost forgotten it, and thereby bringing it back to the interior of the mind. This process is used in many systems including SuperMemo, Anki, and Synap.

Conclusion – Final Words

The Tip of the tongue phenomenon

Have you ever been asked anything that you know the answer to but you still find yourself struggling to think of the exact right word? "Oh I know this one!" you may say, "I know that it begins with a J."

We are all familiar with this kind of sensation. This common state has a name. It is called 'lethologica' or the 'tip of the tongue phenomenon.' The psychologists define this as a feeling, which accompanies comes with the temporary inefficacy of retrieving the information from memory. Although you are aware that you know the answer, the ambiguous information just seems to be out of your mental reach. This kind of feeling can be very annoying when you experience it. However, one of the pros of lethologica is that it lets the researchers analyze various aspects of the memory.

Some of the amusing things which the researchers have discovered about it are:

1. It is universal.

2. The surveys have suggested that about 90% of the speakers in various languages from all across the globe report to have experienced the moments where the memories seem to be momentarily inaccessible.

3. These kinds of moments occur many times and the frequency increases with age.

4. The young people generally have 'tip-of-the-tongue'

moments about once in a week, whereas the older adults find that they may have it at least once every day.

5. People generally remember partial information in bits and pieces.

For instance, they might remember the letter of the word that they are looking for begins with or the no. of syllables of the word.

What's the reason behind this phenomenon?

How do the researchers analyze and clarify lethologica? Language is an immensely complicated process. Most of the time, this course takes places so smoothly that we barely even notice or realize. We think of something, and the brain gives words to show these abstract ideas, and we then speak out what is on our minds. However, since this process is so complicated, several types of things can go wrong, inclusive of the tip-of-the-tongue moments.

When that happens, you may feel that the info is there just outside of your hold. You know that you know it, but it seems temporarily secured and sealed behind some mental brick wall. The moment something finally does bring about the retrieval of the memory, or when somebody else gives the missing info, the relief of those frustrating feelings is tangible.

Why does this happen, though?

Researchers believe that many factors can play a role. However, the exact processes are not completely clear. These events are more apparent to happen when people are just tired. For instance, even though the other feature of the memory like how well the info can be encoded & the presence of any meddling memories can also have access.

The metacognitive clarifications for this phenomenon suggest that the tip-of-the-tongue state acts as kind of an alarm. Like a cautionary signal in your car, these can alert to any hidden issues, which need to be looked at.

As per such theories, these moments are not in & of themselves an issue. Instead, they serve for alerting you that something is going on with retrieval system & it lets you correct the problem. In case you find yourself having this kind of experience constantly before any important presentation or exam, you would then know that you may need to study more for that it remains in the memory for long and deep.

Are there any preventive measures for it?

Some researchers have found that this state can play an adaptive role in the learning and memorizing process. Some of the studies have found that the more time people spend on attending to any of this experience, the better their memory and learning of that material becomes in future. This implies that these moments may result in the stronger encoding of memory, and hence making the retrieval much simpler in the end.

Nonetheless, some other researchers have found out that spending the time in trying to recall the information, which seems to be on the tip of the tongue can be problematic. Even though it may be tempting to spend some time in struggling to find the solution, psychologists Amy Beth Warriner and Karin Humphries suggest that the more time you put in trying to remember one word on the tip of your tongue, there's more likeliness that you will struggle with this word again in future.

What they came to realize is that once people enter this state, it becomes more possible for that state to occur again whenever the person tried to remember that word. Instead of learning the right word, it seems that people learn to go into an incorrect state when they try to get back the word again.

In this study, the researchers displayed thirty participants' questions that they knew, didn't know, or had answers on the tip of their tongues. For the latter-kind answers, the participants were then haphazardly assigned to the groups, which had either ten or thirty seconds to come up with any response. The method was then repeated 2 days later.

The longer the participants spend in that state, the more likely they were to have the similar experience the next time they came across that word. The additional time that the people spend in trying to unearth the word is what the researchers call as the 'incorrect practice' time. Rather than learning the right word, people learn the mistake itself.

In a study done in the year 2015, it was found that this re-occurrence of this phenomenon is possibly a consequence of constant or contained learning, which involves learning of complicated info in incidental ways without any knowledge or understanding that it is learned.

Meaning of the Research

The study has critical applications for educators and students. At the time of the next study session, aim at looking up the right answers instead of trying to recall the information. For the teachers, the study implies that it is more advantageous to give students with the correct answer instead of letting them struggle in recalling it on their own.

What are the ways of preventing future issues following a tip-of-the-tongue event? The best way of breaking the cycle is to repeat that word to you, either aloud or silently. This step created another procedural memory, which aids in minimizing the negative impact of the prior wrong practice.

The good news is that even though these states generally tend to reoccur and are learned, the wrong learning can be corrected either by resolving the issue spontaneously or by using bits of help for triggering the information retrieval. In case you have ever had that evasive answer pop into your head all of a sudden, often when you were not even trying to think about it, then you have experienced the impulsive settlement of lethologica.

Last Tip for Tip-Of-The-Tongue Phenomenon

The tip-of-the-tongue phenomenon can be a feeling of discontent, but it might just be reassuring to know that it is not compulsorily a sign that your memory is declining. These kinds of experiences are common and are, in most of the cases, just a source of annoyance and disappointment. By all means, they can sometimes be very serious in case you experience these at the time of your critical exams or between any important presentations.

The research has suggested that the roots of this phenomenon may be intricate and connected to various causes. You may be more likely to experience it when you are exhausted and tired, or maybe your memory of information was just weak at best. It does not matter what the cause may be, struggling to remember the evasive and ambiguous piece of information may make recalling harder in the future. Rather than struggling to bring forth the memory, only looking up the answer can be more advantageous in resolving your next tip-of-the-tongue experience.

Improving the Memory

A strong memory relies on the vitality and health of your brain. Whether you are a student preparing for your final exams, a working professional concerned about doing all you need to remain mentally sharp, or any senior looking to enhance and preserve your grey matter as you age, there are many things you can do which can improve your mental performance along with your memory.

Final Tips

1. Do not skip your physical exercise - Do not give up on simple aerobics.

2. Exercise your brain - Memory is just like muscles—use it or lose it. Always remember this.

3. Get your Zzz's (sleep well) - Follow your regular sleep schedule.

4. Try to remain stress-free - Take breaks.

5. Make time for your friends - Healthy relationships are the ultimate brain boosters.

6. Eat brain-boosting diets - cut back on caffeine.

7. Laugh - because it is the best medicine.

8. Take practical steps of supporting memory and learning.

9. Treat and identify your health issues.

References

http://idahoptv.org/sciencetrek/topics/brain/facts.cfm

https://lifehacker.com/the-science-behind-how-we-learn-new-skills-908488422

https://www.verywellmind.com/what-is-memory-2795006

https://www.verywellmind.com/explanations-for-forgetting-2795045

https://smallbiztrends.com/2014/11/reasons-we-forget-things.html

https://www.verywellmind.com/memory-retrieval-2795007

https://www.verywellmind.com/what-is-long-term-memory-2795347

http://www.breakthroughlearningcollege.com/memory/visual-memory/

https://study.com/academy/lesson/visual-memory-definition-skills.html

https://www.cognifit.com/science/cognitive-skills/auditory

http://www.breakthroughlearningcollege.com/memory/auditory-memory/

http://www.breakthroughlearningcollege.com/memory/kinesthetic-memory/

http://www.breakthroughlearningcollege.com/memory/mnemonics/

https://www.wikihow.com/Enter-Alpha-State-of-Mind

https://blog.mindvalley.com/accelerated-learning/

https://litemind.com/memory-palace/

http://www.skillstoolbox.com/career-and-education-skills/learning-skills/memory-skills/mnemonics/verbal-mnemonics/

https://www.healthline.com/nutrition/11-brain-foods#section1

https://draxe.com/15-brain-foods-to-boost-focus-and-memory/

https://www.menshealth.com.au/six-super-drinks-to-boost-your-brainpower

https://www.verywellmind.com/how-sugar-affects-the-brain-4065218

https://www.brainhq.com/brain-resources/everyday-brain-fitness/physical-exercise

https://www.health.harvard.edu/blog/regular-exercise-changes-brain-improve-memory-thinking-skills-201404097110

https://www.shape.com/lifestyle/mind-and-body/13-mental-health-benefits-exercise

https://www.maxworkouts.com/articles/entry/4-exercises-that-improve-brain-function

https://onfit.edu.au/health-fitness-blog/the-importance-of-resting-your-mind/

https://www.sleepassociation.org/about-sleep/sleep-hygiene-tips/

https://www.sleepscore.com/caffeine-effect-sleep/

https://www.verywellmind.com/does-caffeine-improve-memory-21846

https://www.neurocorecenters.com/blog/4-common-memory-myths

https://www.independent.co.uk/life-style/health-and-families/sleep-myths-debunked-coffee-tips-snoring-tired-dreams-a8240456.html

https://www.daniel-wong.com/2015/08/17/study-smart/

https://www.cbc.ca/news/technology/exams-studying-tips-brain-science-1.3864360

https://www.wikihow.com/Use-Your-Whole-Brain-While-Studying

http://workwell.unum.com/2018/05/7-ways-keep-mind-sharp-work/

https://www.huffingtonpost.in/entry/work-productivity-hacks_us_56659888e4b079b2818f1f79

https://bebrainfit.com/brain-exercises/

https://www.health.harvard.edu/mind-and-mood/6-simple-steps-to-keep-your-mind-sharp-at-any-age

https://www.psychologytoday.com/intl/articles/200803/pitfalls-perfectionism

https://www.forbes.com/sites/forbescoachescouncil/2018/01/02/why-being-a-perfectionist-can-hold-you-back/#216e0b95d1df

https://www.mindtools.com/pages/article/learn-from-mistakes.htm